In Defense of Doping

In Defense of Doping

Rethinking the level playing field

Alexander Hutchison, PhD

ISBN: 9798883467744

Dedication:

Most of my accomplishments in life can be attributed to the lessons I learned while playing sports. Engaging in sports as an athlete, coach, parent, and fan has shaped my worldview for the better. The lessons of teamwork, merit, resilience, and the acceptance of failure as a pre-requisite for success all came from waking up at five in the morning to get to swim practice on time. I have had the privilege of being coached by some of the finest men and women in the world. But two of my coaches stand out in my mind: my club swim coach in high school, Grant Schmidt, and my coach at the University of Puget Sound, Chris Myhre. Both men exemplify what a coach is supposed to be. They always led by example with a warm, welcoming smile, a firm control of their team, and a willingness to listen when we needed them most. My interactions with Grant and Chris continue to impact every aspect of how I try to live my life as a man, coach, teacher, father, husband, and citizen of this planet we all share. Although I know neither of them agrees with all the opinions I've expressed in this book, they graciously allowed me to honor them in this paragraph. For that, and all the other countless hours of time they spent helping me to become a better person, I am forever in their debt. Grant, Chris, I love you both.

Contents:

Introduction

For years my wife and I discussed taking our daughter to France for a summer vacation. Since we honeymooned in the UK in 2010, we hadn't made a return trip across the pond. In the fall of 2021, I started formulating the idea for this book and began thinking about how wonderful it would be to take a trip to see the event that will play such a prominent role in my story, the Tour de France. I had seen the finish of two stages in 2003 in Bordeaux and Paris, but these were flat stages that played no role in the outcome of the race. What I wanted to see was a mountain stage, and specifically the stage to the alpine ski resort of Alpe d'Huez, one of the most storied summit finishes in all professional cycling. The Tour organizers release the race route for the coming year in early October. With great anticipation, my daughter and I got up early one school-day morning to check the Tour de France website. There it was! The Tour was returning to Alpe d'Huez for the first time in four years. Whatever reservations I'd had about the trip evaporated. Of course, I insisted that this part of the trip would be for research purposes. If I was going to suggest that doping was at least understandable considering the extreme difficulty of the event, I needed to see the toughest the Tour had to offer, up close and personal.

We sat at my computer, hopped onto one of the travel websites and began to schedule everything around the July 14th date of the Alpe d'Huez stage, Bastille Day no less. Before we went to sleep that night, the itinerary was set, the plane tickets purchased, the hotels and car reserved. I even rented a bike to coast down to Bourg-d'Oisans, the village at the base of the Alpe, and ride the famed 21 switchbacks back up to our hotel.

After shaking off our jet lag in a bed and breakfast an hour south of Paris, and three amazing days in Lyon, we made our way to Alpe d'Huez. Driving in the Alps was an unforgettable experience. I've driven over the Rockies,

Cascades, and Sierra Nevadas. Some of the peaks in these American mountain ranges are taller than their French counterparts. But American engineers decided ages ago to make the grades of our mountain roads somewhat gentler than what you find in Europe. The roads in the French Alps are steep and narrow. We drove through Bourg-d'Oisans and began the climb up to Alpe d'Huez. There were cyclists everywhere and their abilities ranged from extremely fit athletes who danced on their pedals as they gently swayed their bikes from side to side, to weekend warriors, like me, who looked like they had recently eaten a little too much of the French cuisine.

Figure 1. How lucky is this? Standing next to the road sign that marks the finish area of the Alpe d'Huez stage with our hotel in the background.

Although we arrived three days before the stage, both shoulders of the road were already filling with fans in their campervans covered in a travelling UN of flags. The aromas of grilled meats wafted through the air alongside the jovial sounds of laughter and music. As we approached the seventh switchback, I told my daughter to get ready to see a lot of people in orange. *"Are they Dutch?"* she asked. Riders from the Netherlands dominated the Alpe d'Huez stage in the early days, winning six of eight visits between 1976 and 1983. To honor their countrymen, a sizable Dutch contingent began gathering at the seventh turn and the tradition stuck.

When we arrived at our hotel, we took some time to enjoy the cool weather and walk around to see what the quaint little village had to offer. Since we were travelling on a budget, our hotel wasn't the most modern. It was obviously designed for skiers who spend their days on the slopes and their evenings passed out in the summer-camp style cots. But the owners were a pleasant older couple who spoke no English, which was perfect because none of us spoke French. I found it humorous how the wife did the same thing that I see most Americans do when they meet a foreigner who doesn't speak the language, she spoke to me very slowly and loudly, in French...

About 20 yards outside the front door of the hotel stood a 15' high wooden sign with the silhouette of a cyclist in yellow with the word *"Arrivée"* etched on it. It dawned on me that this was the finish line. Through absolute dumb luck I had booked us a room at the finish line (Figure 1)!

As the big day neared and the Tour caravan of support vehicles and fans began to flood in, it became clear that the finish line was not at the wooden sign, but literally next to our hotel. As a matter of fact, the gendarmes asked me to move our rental car that I'd parked by the side entrance because it was blocking the portable finishing stage that is setup prior to each finish. If we had wanted to, we could've watched the finish from our fourth-floor balcony.

On the day of the stage, I took my daughter down into the thick of the revelry that precedes the arrival of the cyclists. Dozens of very attractive young men and women in their early 20s toss out free samples of drinks, shirts, and hats, all supplied by the corporate sponsors whose advertising Euros make the event possible. After an hour of running around I wanted to get set in my spot across from the podium, around 100 yards beyond the finish line. My wife and daughter decided they wanted to stay closer to action at the finish line. As Briton, Tom Pidcock made his way to a solo finish, those of us standing across from the podium were watching on a huge

TV screen as the action unfolded between the overall leaders of the race further down the mountain. We all waited for a big attack to come, but it never did.

Unfortunately for me, the decisive attack of the Tour took place the day before during stage 11. The two-time defending champion Tadej Pogačar cracked on the final climb up the Col du Granon, relinquishing the Yellow jersey, worn by the overall leader, to Jonas Vingegaard. During stage 12 to Alpe d'Huez, the two rivals rode side by side the whole day, finishing a few minutes behind Pidcock. I watched as the Yellow, White (Best Young Rider), Green (Best Sprinter), and Polka Dot (King of the Mountains) jerseys rolled past us and quickly disappeared behind the podium to prepare for the awards ceremony. As I stood behind the barricades clapping, I was aware of several camera crews. What I didn't know was that one of those crews was filming for a Netflix docuseries titled *The Tour de France Unchained*. If you want to confirm my story you can see me during episode five at the 34:07 mark. I'm flanked by a little a boy on my left with green sunglasses and a yellow cap, and a woman wearing a white surgical mask to my right. My 270 lbs. frame, white goatee, and yellow and white trucker cap look more suited to a college tailgate party than the Superbowl of cycling.

A few minutes later my wife and daughter joined me as we watched the awards ceremony for the stage win and the four jerseys. While waiting we got to see the post-race rituals of several of the riders. One team camped no more than two feet in front of us and began guzzling sodas and eating handfuls of Haribo gummy bears. My daughter asked why they would eat candy instead of one of the many high-priced sports nutrition snacks that we regularly see at many of the running races that we do as a family. I told her that the one thing they all needed right now was a lot of sugar to replenish their stores that had been depleted from their livers and muscles during the stage. Because they were so fit, the term *"junk food"* didn't apply to them. They would have a nutritious meal later.

As I watched this group of four teammates scarf down their recovery candies, I noticed something on the crook of the elbow of one of the cyclists, an unmistakable red puncture

Figure 2. With my family in front of the A-frame of honor.

mark on his median cubital vein, the big vein in the middle of the elbow. Having collected hundreds of blood samples during my dissertation and post-doctoral fellowship, I know what it looks like when a vein has been poked a few too many times. A quick scan of the three other men in the group revealed a puffy-red-purple mark on the inner elbow of two of his teammates. Surprised by what I was seeing, I not-so-subtly nudged my wife and pointed to their arms. She provided a non-verbal acknowledgement with a wide-eyed look, as if to say, *"What the hell?"* Their soigneur (team assistant) who had provided them with their gummy bears and sodas noticed us gawking at their arms and quickly hustled them away. Considering how unusually hot it was in France in the summer of 2022, the most likely explanation for the needle marks was that these men had received at least one intravenous infusion of fluids to hasten their rehydration and recovery. But the World Antidoping Agency (WADA) and all the sports that follow its regulations, including the international governing body of cycling, the Union Cyclist Internationale (UCI), banned the use of IV infusions of more than 100ml/12 hours in 2018, a volume too small to rehydrate anyone [1]. The reason for the rule is that cycling has a long history of athletes using IV fluids to dilute their blood to hide the signs of blood boosting products that increase the number of red blood cells, which provide a significant competitive advantage. So, at best this team was breaking the relatively new rule for what I think is a justifiable reason, efficient rehydration after several hours of exertion in extreme heat while riding up mountains that our rental car struggled to climb.

Because part of my motivation for taking this trip was to collect information for a book about doping, I felt vindicated (and a little happy) to see that even now, during our current era of *"clean sport"*, that it had been so easy to find evidence of riders breaking anti-doping rules. And why should anyone be surprised? The race is just as grueling as it ever has been, maybe more. Suffering is suffering no matter how many race organizers, governing bodies, and fans wag their fingers of judgement at the peloton as it grinds its way around a country roughly the size of Texas. The DNA of today's professional cyclists hasn't evolved much since the race was first competed in 1903 when athletes would take almost anything to ease their pain. Brandy, beer, wine, cocaine, and opium were some of the lighter substances used in those early days. But harder drugs like ether, nitroglycerine, and even strychnine were frequently used performance enhancing drugs (PED).

Unfortunately, I never got to ride up Alpe d'Huez. The original plan was to hop on my rental bike shortly after arriving and before the crowds got too heavy. But an ill-advised stop at a crepe shop triggered a food allergy that kept me close to the bathroom for several hours after our arrival. The backup plan was to try again the day after the stage. But being the first time that Covid restrictions had been completely lifted for the Tour in two years, the crowds were bigger than expected and the road had been left a mess. The gendarmes were forced to close it for cleaning. We had to move on to our next stop on our vacation. The closest that I got to riding on Alpe d'Huez was taking a family photo on a set of old Peugeots that were mounted in front of a wall of plaques with the names of all the individual stage winners who had ridden their way into the pantheon of cycling (Figure 2). After we took our photo, I scanned the names on the wall. I was looking for two blank slates for the years 2001 and 2004 when Lance Armstrong was first to the summit. The organizers of the Tour de France had long-since declared that because so many cyclists had been involved in doping during Armstrong's seven-year reign, it would be impossible to find a clean athlete to declare a winner for any of those years. Their solution was to declare this an era of darkness during which there was no official winner.

But the people who controlled this wall had a different idea for how to respond to the Armstrong era. The plaques weren't blank, instead they contained the name of Jan Ulrich, Armstrong's closest rival, and a confirmed doper. In 2013 Ulrich admitted to using PED during much of his career. I quickly recognized the names of several other men who had also been caught up in doping scandals but hadn't been stripped of their place in history. Of the 25 individual names on that wall, 13 belonged to men who had either admitted to doping, tested positive, or had been implicated in doping investigations. For most of these men the admission of guilt prompted at least some degree of humility and remorse. But that wasn't the case for the first, and in my opinion, most legendary name on the Alpe d'Huez wall of honor.

Italian Fausta Coppi won the first visit to Alpe d'Huez in 1952 on his way to winning his second Tour. The first true international superstar of the sport, Coppi was also the first to win both the Giro d'Italia (the second most important grand tour of cycling) and the Tour de France in the same year, accomplishing the feat twice in 1949 and 1952. For his career Coppi won two Tours, five Giros, four of the five spring classic races, one world championship, and he also held the world hour-record from 1942 to 1956. In his book *Fallen Angel, The Passion of Fausto Coppi*, William Fotheringham wrote:

> Coppi was overt about his use of stimulants, which were not banned until five years after his death [in 1960]. His comments to the radio reporter Mario Ferretti that he only used drugs *'when necessary'* is now widely quoted, with the caveat that it was *'almost always'* necessary. He explained to Rino Negri [Italian journalist]: *'I'm a professional. If I could discover a medicine which didn't damage my heart and nervous system, I wouldn't hesitate to use it to win, and often.'* [2]

Prior to the implementation of the first antidoping rules in 1965, cyclists in general, and certainly the stars of the sport weren't afraid to admit to using whatever methods they deemed necessary to make it from one hellish race to another. The man who replaced Coppi as the boss of the peloton, Frenchman Jacques Anquetil, the first man to win the Tour five times, regularly shared his disdain for being questioned about the ethics of doping.

After he'd written the articles in which he said, *"I dope because everybody dopes,"* he was interviewed on television later in the winter with the sports minister who told him off and said to him that declarations like that could lead to confusion. Anquetil replied, *"You're sports minister, and yet you think I rode Bordeaux-Paris using just sugar."* From Sex, Lies, and Handlebar Tape, The Remarkable Life of Jacque Anquetil, by Paul Howard [3].

"You'd have to be an imbecile or hypocrite to imagine that a professional cyclist who rides 235 days a year can hold himself together without stimulants." Velopedia, The Infographic Book of Cycling, by Robert Dineen [4].

Despite these full-throated admissions, and perhaps because of them, cycling fans maintain a level of respect, and even reverence for these pioneering superstars that doesn't exist for the men who followed them, particularly Lance Armstrong. It's a fascinating contradiction. Although all confirmed dopers from the EPO era, i.e., 1990-2010, have faced some level of public scorn, none have been treated like Armstrong. For example, in 1996 Bjarne Riis dominated the Tour, ending the reign of another five-time champion, Miguel Indurain. During the decisive 16th stage that finished at the summit of the famed Hautacam in the Pyrenees, Riis toyed with the opposition in a manner similar to what Armstrong would do to consolidate his lead in the 1999 Tour three years later. So dominant was Riis' performance that he was later given the nickname *"Mr. 60%"*, a euphemism alluding to the amount of oxygen-carrying red blood cells in his body. Without taking EPO, a blood boosting hormone and the PED of choice for most of the peloton during this time, the blood of most men contains between 42%-48% RBC, with the rest being plasma. On May 25, 2007, while the manager of one of the best cycling teams in the world, Team CSC, Riis admitted to taking several PED during his career. Instead of being shunned by the sport, or society in general, he continued his coaching career, directing wins in four grand tours, two Tours de France (2008 and 2010), one Giro d'Italia (2006), and the 2012 Vuelta a España (the third of the grand tours) [5]. He remains the official winner of the 1996 Tour and is a respected team manager.

Riis preceded Lance Armstrong in the professional peloton by six years. Although he has never revealed who directed his doping plan it is widely believed to have been Dr. Francesco Conconi, the mentor and colleague of Dr. Michele Ferrari, who developed Armstrong's doping plan. The lessons learned while making Riis a champion were perfected to make Armstrong the only seven-time Tour winner. The chapter on Lance Armstrong in the book of doping history could not have been written without Bjarne Riis. So why is Armstrong treated with disdain while Riis, Coppi, Anquetil, and so many other doped winners are venerated? As I see it there are two reasons: 1) Armstrong is not European, and 2) he won the Tour seven consecutive times, two more than anyone else. Had he been born on the continent, or only won once or twice, perhaps Armstrong could have maintained his place in the official history of the Tour de France. But having a brash, irreverent, bratty American as the most decorated rider in Tour de France history was too much for the French, and Europeans in general, to stomach. After all, in the long history of the race only two non-Europeans have ever officially won the Tour; American, Greg LeMond and Columbian, Egan Bernal.

Perhaps my position is naïve and overly simplistic. There's no question that Armstrong behaved like a monstrous bully who did his best to ruin the lives of anyone who spoke out against him. But many other Tour champions embraced vices and bad behavior. Coppi and his mistress Guilia Occhini were put on trial for adultery during a time when divorce was illegal in Italy [2]. So scandalous was the affair that Pope Pius XII personally asked Coppi to return to his wife and when he did not, the Pope refused to bless the Giro d'Italia for as long as Coppi was a participant.

Not to be outdone, Anquetil had an affair with Jeanine Boëda, the wife of his doctor, betraying a man who for years had been an adoring fan and friend [3]. After they married Anquetil wanted to have more children, but Jeanine couldn't.

They debated about the possibility of hiring a surrogate, but Jeanine didn't like the idea of her husband impregnating a stranger, which of course makes perfect sense. Instead, they settled on a compromise that didn't make any sense at all. Jeanine asked her 18-year-old daughter, Anquetil's stepdaughter Annie, to bear a child that would be both her daughter and step-sister. Even after the birth of Anquetil and Annie's daughter, Sophie in 1971, they maintained a sexual relationship for another 12 years. Whatever Lance Armstrong did, and he did a lot, nothing compares to openly carrying on an incestuous love triangle with your wife and stepdaughter. Yet, Armstrong is still *persona non grata* while Coppi and Anquetil are worshipped, not just as sportsmen, but as great men.

This disproportionate response to how we judge our fallen heroes is something that I have struggled to understand for many years, and it is one of the reasons that I decided to write this book. What I hope to convey is that doping is rarely a clear-cut issue. What is considered doping in one sport can be an accepted method of coping with an injury in another. Some athletes test positive for miniscule amounts of drugs after consuming contaminated supplements, food, or legally prescribed drugs. Although the amounts found in their bodies are often too small to provide any competitive advantage, the 'offending' athletes are often punished just the same as if they had intended to cheat. Others have been disqualified for taking recreational drugs that provide no performance enhancing benefit whatsoever, e.g., marijuana or ecstasy. Even when athletes dope with intent, there are obvious, understandable reasons for their actions, e.g., money, pride, and a desperate desire to maintain an occupation for which they have spent a lifetime training. These behaviors are not unique to athletes. Many average people regularly take drugs to enhance their performance at work, in the classroom, or in their personal lives. However, many of these same people are the first to turn on their sporting heroes when they behave similarly. It is a classic case of *'do as I say and not as I do.'*

My hope is that after reading this book you will have a better understanding of both what it means to dope and why many athletes choose to do so. Sport is a metaphor for life, and more often than not life exists on a spectrum of choices and behaviors far away from the binary code of right and wrong. To the contrary, life is filled with nuance, and nuance is messy.

Reference:

1. *TUE Physician Guidelines: Intravenous Infusions and/or Injections*, W.A.D.A. (WADA), Editor. 2018.
2. Fotheringham, W., *Fallen Angel: The Passion of Fausto Coppi*. 2010, London, England, UK: Yellow Jersey Press.
3. Howard, P., *Sex, Lies, and Handlebar Tape: The Remarkable Life of Jacques Anquetil, The First Five-Times Winner of the Tour de France*. 2011, Edinburgh, Scotland, UK: Mainstream Publishing Company.
4. Dineen, R., *Velopedia: The Infographic Book of Cycling*. 2017, London, England, UK: Aurum Press.
5. Riis, B., *RIIS: Stages of Light and Dark*. 2012, Copenhagen, Denmark: People's Press.

Chapter 1. What is doping?

"If you're a dope like me, you get every sports channel you can get. I'm watching, you know, Netherlands soccer." — ***Michael Keaton***

Although the desire to enhance athletic performance likely dates to the creation of athletic competition during prehistory, the earliest reference to the word "doping" in relation to sport didn't occur until the end of the 19th century. The word "dop" was originally the name of a primitive alcoholic drink that was a described as being something like a combination of mead and wine, but with a hefty stimulatory kick. Zulu and Bantu warriors of South Africa would drink the concoction before religious ceremonies, rites of passage, and battle [1]. White settlers including Afrikaans and Dutch called the drink "doop". The modern definition used by anti-doping authorities is any substance or method used to gain an unfair advantage in athletics. Before I defend my central thesis, that many of the practices that we call doping are at least understandable, if not reasonable, I need to define the specific drugs and techniques that will appear in later chapters.

Anabolic steroids

Anabolism means to build something large from smaller subunits. It is the opposite of catabolism, which means to break down a big thing into its smaller component parts. In this case proteins are built from amino acids. Proteins are then assembled into muscles which we use to move. The best-known anabolic steroid is testosterone. Both men and women produce testosterone, with men producing 20-70X more than women. Testosterone levels peak in the early twenties, remain level until around 30, and then decline at a relatively constant rate over the rest of life. Testosterone levels spike after exercise, allowing the body to recover from the workout by repairing muscle tissue that is damaged during exercise, and under the right conditions, adding new muscle. Testosterone is also an androgenic hormone, meaning that it helps produce secondary sexual characteristics during puberty including hair growth on the face, armpits, and groin, production of sebaceous oils on the skin, and deepening of the voice.

In addition to testosterone there are dozens of synthetic anabolic steroids that have similar chemical structures to testosterone but varying degrees of anabolic and androgenic properties. The ideal synthetic anabolic hormone is one that stimulates a lot of muscle growth but has few androgenic properties, especially for women. Nothing gives away steroid use in women faster than a five o'clock shadow. The other reason that synthetic anabolic steroids are of interest is that each change in the chemical structure has the potential for making the new synthetic steroid undetectable to drug testers. This is what happened during the late 1990s when the Bay Area Laboratory Cooperative (BALCO) began distributing a newly develop anabolic steroid that they called *the clear* [2]. The only reason that drug testers were able to develop a test for *the clear* was because an anonymous whistleblower sent USADA a syringe containing the new PED.

Chronic illicit use of anabolic steroids can result in several nasty side effects. First, when we take exogenous hormones our bodies say, "hey if you're already injecting all of this extra testosterone (insert any other hormone here), then I don't need to keep producing so much." In this case, the testicles shrink, and sperm count drops significantly. This is reversible but often requires additional hormone therapy to jump start endogenous production. The more severe side effects can include erectile dysfunction, hair loss on the head, excessive hair growth everywhere else, and severe acne. Men can experience breast development while women can experience breast shrinkage. Women can experience growth of hair on the face and body, enlargement of the clitoris, deepening of the voice, and complications with menstruation and fertility. Anabolic hormones also increase the production of red blood cells, thickening the blood to the point that blood clots may form. Blood clots increase the risk of heart attack and stroke. Thicker blood can also increase blood pressure, straining the kidneys and other major organs. Finally, chronic steroid use can impact emotions. Aggressive behavior, mood swings and paranoia are frequently reported by steroid users.

Erythropoietin (EPO)

EPO is a hormone that stimulates the bone marrow to make more red blood cells (RBC). RBC carry oxygen from the lungs to the rest of the body. Since we need oxygen to live, maintaining adequate RBC levels is a critical function for survival. We regularly replace RBC as they get worn out and this requires a steady supply of EPO to be present in the blood. But there are times when oxygen levels drop either because we lose RBC, (a severe bleed, anemia, or menstruation), or there is less oxygen in the air we breathe, (when we travel from low to high altitude). In response to these conditions, EPO levels spike until oxygen levels return to normal. In addition to these more normal occurrences, there are two other examples of reduced RBC levels that happen because of disease, i.e., kidney failure and as a side effect of chemotherapy. EPO is made by the kidneys, so when they begin to fail, EPO production can decrease. One side effect of chemotherapy is the destruction of bone marrow. Synthetic EPO was developed to treat anemia related to kidney failure and cancer. As a PED, EPO increases the amount of oxygen that is delivered to the muscles during high intensity exercise. This is critical to success in endurance activities like distance running and cycling. EPO can improve athletic performance by as much as 10%, this represents the difference between winning the Tour de France and finishing last.

Unlike most other drugs on banned substances lists, there is ample scientific evidence for the performance enhancing properties of anabolic steroids and EPO. If an athlete is caught taking either of these drugs, they're doing so to enhance their performance, and not to either heal an injury or numb their pain. These drugs are taken to win, not stay alive.

The big side effect of EPO use is thickening of the blood that can result in clots, heart attack, and stroke. In the early years of the EPO era of cycling there were several reports of young riders dying in their sleep when their syrupy blood stopped their hearts. Although none of these deaths were definitively linked to EPO use, there's no other plausible reason why 30+ healthy, young, professional athletes would die in their 20s and 30s from heart failure.

Cortisone

Cortisone is one of a class of synthetic steroid hormones called corticosteroids. The natural analog that we produce is called cortisol, and it is released by the adrenal glands in response to stress. Cortisone is prescribed to reduce inflammation and can be applied to the skin in a cream, taken orally as a pill, or injected into the muscles or joints. As a PED, cortisone is a potent stimulator of the central nervous system, reducing the sensations of pain and fatigue and increasing awareness. But, when applied to the skin or injected into a joint, very little cortisone makes it into circulation, greatly reducing its potential as a PED. Because of this, several sports allow for intra-articular (into joints) injections of cortisone to reduce inflammation and pain resulting from either acute or chronic injury.

Because corticosteroids reduce the inflammatory response, they also impair immune function, leaving chronic users more prone to infections. Other side effects include weight gain, weakening of the bones, increased risk of developing cataracts and glaucoma, and insomnia.

Human Growth Hormone (HGH)

Just like it sounds, HGH stimulates growth in just about every tissue in the body. Logically, HGH levels peak around age 10 and then rapidly fall over the next ten years, leveling off by the time we get to 40-50 years. Children who suffer from HGH deficiency experience stunted growth. Deficient adults have more body fat and less muscle. HGH is often taken with anabolic steroids to augment muscle gains and reduce body fat. More importantly, HGH is believed to increase the growth rate of soft tissues including tendons and cartilage which are frequently injured by the unnaturally large (steroid-induced) muscles to which they are attached.

Chronic use of HGH can lead to nerve, muscle, and joint damage, water retention in muscles and joints, elevated cholesterol, and increased incidence of diabetes and certain cancers.

Diuretics

Diuretics are drugs that reduce the volume of fluid (plasma) in your blood by making you urinate more frequently and with greater volume. By decreasing the volume of blood in the circulatory system, diuretics decrease chronically high blood pressure. Diuretics have no performance enhancing properties, but they act as what are called masking agents. In other words, diuretics mask the use of other PED by flushing them out of the body before they can be detected or by diluting the urine to the point where the PED is less likely to be detected.

The most reported side effect of excessive use of diuretics is dehydration, not something endurance athletes want to deal with during a race. Because diuretics remove water from circulation, abuse can lead to the removal of key electrolytes including sodium, potassium, magnesium, and chlorine. Major alterations in blood chemistry can have dire impacts on electrical transmissions, impacting the nervous system and the heart.

Clenbuterol

Clenbuterol was developed as a decongestant and bronchodilator. It relaxes the muscles around the bronchiole tubes, allowing air to flow more freely. But clenbuterol has several PED properties: it alters body composition, reducing body fat and possibly increasing muscle mass. Like cortisone, clenbuterol is also a potent stimulator of the nervous system, increasing awareness and reducing the sensations of pain and fatigue.

Since clenbuterol stimulates the nervous system, chronic use can lead to insomnia, paranoia, tremors, and shakiness, vomiting and nausea, elevated body temperature, sweating, anxiety, and muscle cramps.

Amphetamines

Amphetamines, as a general class of drug, were first synthesized as early as 1887 and were first marketed as decongestants in 1933. They became widely used by both the Allied and Axis forces during World War II. Amphetamines have two modes of action as PED: they stimulate the central nervous system and reduce inhibitory signals of pain, heat, and fatigue.

The side effects of amphetamines are like those of clenbuterol. Constantly revving up the metabolism alters brain function, leading to insomnia, anxiety, and teeth grinding. Other effects include extreme weight loss, hypertension, and irregular/elevated heart rate.

The Donkey and the Thoroughbred Myth

One of the most frequent condemnations of doping is that is represents a "short cut" that makes it easier for the dopers to achieve their athletic goals. In cycling parlance this is called turning a donkey into a thoroughbred. Although I understand the sentiment behind this position, it's not quite right. The most effective PED, namely steroids and HGH, are used during training and not during competition. Both work by improving the quality of recovery and how quickly it occurs after exercise. Recovery is an umbrella term that includes several physiological changes that must happen within the body before someone can expect for their next bout of exercise to occur at peak performance. The length of the recovery period is dependent on several factors including the intensity of the exercise, the duration of the exercise, the quality of the nutrients consumed during and between sessions, and the hormonal status of the athlete.

As exercise intensity and duration increase, the recovery period gets longer. During exercise we burn fuels stored in our muscles and liver that must be replenished. We also cause damage to the muscles and bones that must be repaired and even added to if strength gains are to occur. The physiological signals that drive fuel restoration and tissue repair are driven by a series of hormones including testosterone and HGH. Just as important as their ability to make athletes bigger, anabolic steroids and HGH reduce recovery time. With recovery time shortened, doped athletes can increase the intensity, duration, and frequency of their workouts. This is the exact opposite of a short cut; it's taking the long way home. Doped athletes can do more work than can clean athletes.

Shortly after the Berlin Wall was built in 1961, the German Democratic Republic (GDR) began a campaign to use sports as a means of gaining international recognition. In his book *Faust's Gold*, Steven Ungerleider provides a thorough history of the development of State Plan Topic 14.25, the GDR's national sports model that identified young talent, sent them to sports boarding schools, and systematically doped its athletes with several performance enhancing drugs, the most important of which being a synthetic anabolic steroid developed in the GDR called Oral Turinobol [3]. Depending on your perspective, the crowning achievement of this scheme came during the 1976 Montreal Summer Olympics when the GDR, with a population of around 18 million, finished second in the medal count behind only the Soviet Union. In the swimming competition where 13 events were competed, the East German women won 11 gold, six silver, and a bronze.

In 1993, four years after the fall of the Berlin wall, and three years after reunification with West Germany began, records related to State Plan Topic 14.25 were released to the public. The documents contained the training plans for all Olympic sports including swimming. What stood out was the incredible training volume that the swimmers were able to maintain, year after year. A conservative estimate is that training volume, calculated as the total distance swum in meters, was between 10%-15% more than any other country competing. Being able to train that hard for that long, and that regularly allowed the GDR swimmers to get faster than was naturally possible.

Let me be clear, I condemn the actions of the GDR and all other countries who either doped their athletes without their knowledge or coerced them to comply. My only point is that doping is not taking the easy way out. Dopers end up working harder than either they or their clean competitors could without PED. Some athletes who won their events while doping likely could have done so without PED, but they would not have won by as big a margin. However, most who dope could never achieve the same heights in their respective sports, no matter how hard they trained. Doping allows humans to exceed the limits of their physiology. Whatever your position on doping, understand that PED do not represent laziness in sport. To the contrary, as much as it pains me to say so, in most instances taking PED represents an athlete's willingness to do anything and everything necessary to perform at their absolute best. Many take the position that no one who dopes can claim to be performing at the best of their abilities because those abilities have been synthetically enhanced. Others look at doping as another means to an end, just like using the most modern technological advancements in equipment to go faster, jump higher, and hit harder. Like most things in life, it comes down to perspective. If you've never had a multimillion-dollar contract on the line, you may not be able to empathize with someone facing the decision of whether or not to dope. Remember, sport is a metaphor for life, and like life, the morality of sports can be messy. As you read this book, come back to this point. What would you do if faced with some of the scenarios that I will present?

Reference:

1. Conti, A.A., *Doping in sports in ancient and recent times*. Med Secoli, 2010. **22**(1-3): p. 181-90.
2. Mark Fainaru-Wada, L.W., *Game of Shadows*. 2006, Sheridan, Wyoming, USA: Gotham Books.
3. Ungerleider, S., *Faust's Gold: Inside the East German Doping Machine*. 2013, New York, New York, USA: St. Martin's Press.

Chapter 2: Money makes the world go round.

"The answer to all your question is... Money" — ***Don Ohlmeyer, NBC Producer***

When pitching this book to friends and family, the most asked question was some version of the following: *"So, you think athletes should be able to take anything they want... no rules?"* The question conjures memories of watching an SNL Weekend Update from the All-Drug Olympics. The inspiration for the skit, which aired on October 8, 1988, was the disqualification of Canadian sprinter Ben Johnson from the Seoul Summer Olympics. His post-race urine sample contained anabolic steroids. What should have been a story about the climax of his five-year rivalry with American sprinter Carl Lewis, quickly degenerated into a tabloid-ready soap opera. After being robbed of such a great story, many Americans, including me, needed a good laugh.

The mock-news story takes place in the host city of the All-Drug Olympics, Bogota, Columbia, of course. Weekend Update news anchor Dennis Miller introduces the story.

> *"In response to what its sponsors claim is an idea whose time has come, the first All-Drug Olympics opened today in Bogota, Columbia. Athletes are allowed to take any substance whatsoever before, after, and even during the competition. So far, 115 world records have been shattered! We go now to correspondent Kevin Nealon, live in Bogota for the Weightlifting Finals. Kevin?"*
>
> Sports correspondent, Kevin Nealon is standing in front of the Soviet Union's Sergei Akmudov who is about to attempt a lift in the clean and jerk.

"[Akmudov's] trainer has told me that he's taken anabolic steroids, Novocain, Nyquil, Darvon, and some sort of fish paralyzer. Also, I believe he's had a few cocktails within the last hour or so. All of this is, of course, perfectly legal at the All-Drug Olympics, in fact it's encouraged. Akmudov is getting set now, he's going for a clean and jerk of over 1500 pounds, which would triple the existing world record. That's an awful lot of weight, Dennis, and here he goes."

The camera focuses on Akmudov who is already in position, squatting with his arms gripping the bar. He bears down, letting out a carnal yawp. With one last scream he yanks himself up, ripping both arms from their sockets while his hands remain gripping the bar. Akmudov looks both confused and disappointed, blood squirts from his shoulders where his arms once were.

"Oh! He pulled his arms off! He's pulled his arms off, that's gotta be disappointing to the big Russian! You know, you hate to see something like this happen, Dennis! He probably doesn't have that much pain right now, but I think tomorrow he's really gonna feel that. Dennis! Back to you!

Obviously, this is not the dystopian hellscape that I wish for athletics. Sport cannot be allowed to recede into the wild west that existed before the first doping control tests began in many sports in the 1960s. But the permissible uses of some key substances and techniques are too few and the punishments too draconian. To better understand what it is that I am advocating, it is important to understand the definition of a banned substance or practice as per WADA regulations. The criteria for inclusion of a substance, a class of substances, or a method in the prohibited list requires that any one of the following three criteria be met: 1) potential to enhance performance, 2) risk for the athletes' health, or 3) violation of the spirit of sport. Let's break these down one at a time.

Potential to enhance performance

Although it seems like this should be easy to determine, in many cases, particularly when it comes to recreational drugs, the process is anything but simple. To test a substance or method for its efficacy in enhancing athletic performance, you first must design a study and get a university or research institute to allow you to test it on human subjects. Any university or institute that engages in human subjects' research has a committee called an Internal Review Board (IRB) for the Protection of Human Subjects, tasked with making sure that the protocol to be used in the study is ethical and that the risks associated with the study design are balanced against the potential knowledge to be gained. Because of this, a research project to determine whether amphetamines improve cycling speed in a one-hour time trial is likely to be rejected.

Then there's the matter of determining which element of a sport to test. For example, to be an excellent football player you need speed, strength, agility, hand-eye coordination, nimble feet, and both aerobic and anaerobic fitness. Depending on which position you play on the field, you may need more or fewer of any of these elements, and in different combinations. How does any single study test all these characteristics for all types of athletes? It's not possible. But that's why the criterion is written as it is, i.e., the potential to enhance performance.

Now, let's add to this the fact that there are currently more than 200 substances on the banned list (growing every year), and it becomes an impossible task to test all of them in every way necessary to conclusively state that each of these substances is a performance enhancer. This is before we even discuss who is going to pay for these studies. Large granting agencies are interested in advancing our knowledge of basic science for the purpose of improving the lives of our citizens, not making athletes bigger, faster, and stronger.

Lastly, if you don't know whether or not a drug improves athletic performance, then you obviously don't know how much of the drug has to be present in the blood or urine in order for it to have any impact. This question arises when positive tests result from contamination of food or legally prescribed drugs, or when a banned substance is an active but unlabeled ingredient in an over-the-counter supplement. Although I agree that the final burden falls to the athletes to know what they are putting into their bodies, if the banned substance is consumed in such miniscule amounts that it can't possibly improve athletic performance, the punishment shouldn't be the same as when an athlete cheats with intent.

Risk for the athletes' health

Again, sounds simple, doesn't it? Not really. For each substance in question, you must know the dosage and frequency of consumption. Most published drug studies used to make these determinations were conducted using average mortals as test subjects, not uber healthy, elite athletes who likely metabolize and clear the drugs faster. But more importantly, lots of substances that we think of as innocuous can cause harm depending on the circumstances. For example, exercise-associated hyponatremia is a common medical complication experienced during long-distance racing (marathon, ultramarathon, and triathlon) and has been a cause of race-related fatalities. The term hyponatremia means *"too little"* (hypo) *"sodium in the blood"* (natremia). It is caused by a combination of excessive sweating and over-consumption of water, that results in diluted blood. Messing up the electrolyte balance of the blood can have severe consequences, altering conduction of electrical impulses throughout the body. This impacts the muscles, heart, and brain. The best way to avoid this during an event is to swallow some salt tablets before, during, and after the event, and to drink fluids that contain electrolytes, e.g., Gatorade and Powerade.

I want to be clear that I am not making light of the potential dangers posed by an athlete taking drugs, outside the care of a qualified physician, to improve athletic performance. This is a serious issue, and I am neither advocating for nor condoning the practice. Nor am I being glib when I explain that even water, under certain extreme circumstances, can cause harm. I am, however, making the point that most things can be labelled as potentially dangerous substances.

Violation of the spirit of sport

This brings us to my least favorite of the three criteria. If, somehow, the substance or practice in question doesn't meet either of the previous two criteria, WADA can always fall back on this one, the catch-all criteria. The following is from the WADA code (2021).

> *"Anti-doping programs seek to preserve what is intrinsically valuable about sport. This intrinsic value is often referred to as "the spirit of sport." It is the essence of Olympism, the pursuit of human excellence through the dedicated perfection of each person's talents. It is how we play true. The spirit of sport is the celebration of the human spirit, body, and mind, and is reflected in values we find in and through sport, including ethics, fair play, honesty, health, excellence in performance, character and education, fun and joy,*

teamwork, dedication and commitment, respect for rules and laws, respect for self and other participants, courage, community and solidarity."

The characterization of sports as intrinsically ethical, honest, and fair is debatable at best. If sports were inherently fair, there would be no need to establish rules beyond the basics of how to play each game. To the contrary, looking back through the histories of many major sports reveals them to be anything but safe, fair, diverse, or equitable.

- The earliest iteration of American football was a brutal, bloody game that was responsible for at least 37 deaths between 1904 and 1905. The carnage prompted President Theodore Roosevelt to threaten to ban the game altogether if it were not regulated and made safer, hastening the eventual establishment of the National Collegiate Athletics Association (NCAA).
- Major League Baseball was segregated until Jackie Robinson's rookie season of 1947. Before then, black players could only play in the Negro League (1920-1951).
- The Boston Marathon was a men-only event until Katherine Switzer became the first woman to officially finish the race in 1967. But she had to endure the indignity of being physically assaulted by race organizer, Jock Semple, who ran after her, grabbing her bib, and screaming: *"Get the hell out of my race and give me those numbers!"*
- The first Olympic marathon was competed in 1904 with only male runners. The first Olympic women's marathon was not contested until 1984. Prior to this, our childbearing sisters were considered too frail and delicate to survive 26.2 miles of running.

- For decades, Olympic distance swimming was segregated into two events by gender. The men competed in the 1500m, while women could only race the shorter, 800m. This lasted until 2021 when the Tokyo Olympics finally included a men's 800m and women's 1500m.
- But this inherently sexist, and unfair practice of making the women's events easier, and thus, lesser, continues in track and field where men compete in the decathlon (10 separate events), while the women are relegated to the heptathlon (seven events). Apparently, women still can't handle adding the 400m, discus, and pole vault.
- Women's tennis matches are the best of three sets, while the men play best of five. Serena Williams, Martina Navratilova, and Bill Jean King obviously didn't have the stamina to play two more sets.

It is ironic that WADA invokes the ideal of Olympism as the foundation for the purity of sport. The modern Olympic movement began with the 1896 games in Athens, Greece with an all-male field of 241 athletes who were predominately white. This disparity continues today. The US contingent to the 2018 Winter Olympics was 92% white, and only recently has the participation of men and women approached parity, Tokyo 2020 was 48.8% women [1].

Beyond the glaring inequities in participation related to race and gender, there is the long history of the Olympic games serving as the battlefield for a series of never-ending proxy wars between rival nations. The first example of this was the 1936 Berlin Olympics, when Adolph Hitler showcased his *"master race"* of white, Aryan superhumans. Thankfully Jesse Owens, a black American from the Jim Crow south, dominated the track & field events, winning four golds. Many more examples followed. In 1980, in a misguided response to the Soviet Union's invasion of Afghanistan, President Jimmy Carter boycotted the summer games held in Moscow. As payback, the Soviets and 13 other Eastern Bloc communist nations boycotted the 1984 Los Angeles games. The nadir of the Olympics being used as a stage for international politics was the 1972 games in Munich, when 11 Israeli athletes and coaches were taken hostage and murdered by five members of a Palestinian terrorist group. In each case the spirit of sport was eclipsed by different human agendas that had nothing to do with fair play.

But we don't need such extreme examples to observe how humans regularly make sports unfair. All we must do is look at the influence of wealth (and the lack thereof) on

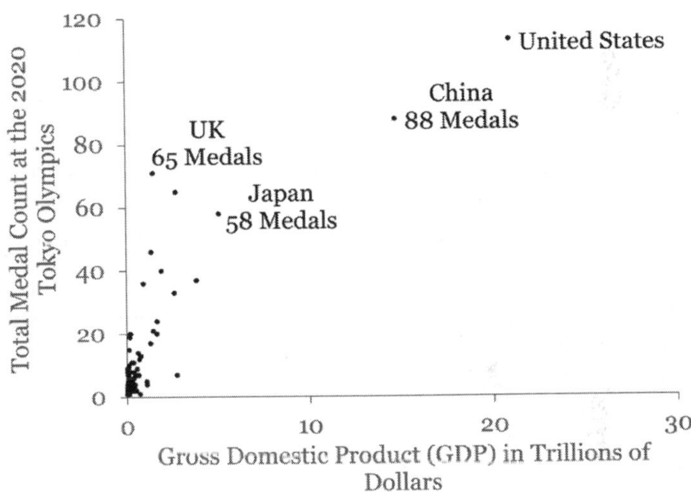

Figure 3. Total medals won during the 2020 Olympics as a function of national GDP in trillions of dollars. There were 88 countries that won medals.

athletic performance, a glaring inequity that runs through all levels of competition. When comparing the gross domestic product (GDP) of all the nations that participated in the 2020 Tokyo Olympics, the richest nations won the most medals (Figure 3) [2]. Indeed, this correlation was 0.83, a perfect correlation is 1.

Participation in recreational sports at the turn of the 20th century was predominantly reserved for people of means who could afford to be amateur athletes. Poor and middle-class people didn't, and often still don't, have time to practice and compete because they have to work longer hours than their wealthier counterparts, in jobs that often require manual labor. This disparity continues in adult *"hobby"* sports in the U.S. like triathlon (a combined 2% of participants are black, Hispanic, Asian, or some other ethnic minority) [3], and swimming (72.8% white) [4]. But even in youth athletics (e.g., soccer, football, basketball, baseball/softball), where the collective distribution of participants more closely matches the proportion of each race in the population, there is still a huge difference in access to the best equipment, facilities, and coaches. These differences are particularly evident at the high school and college levels.

In my home state of Texas, where football is king, over the last 20 years, wealthier suburban school districts have engaged in a bond-funded arms race, building football stadiums that rival some at the highest level of collegiate athletics. I witnessed this firsthand after being hired as the head swimming coach at Southlake Carroll high school in 2001. That fall, the district opened its 12,600-seat stadium at a cost $15 million ($26.3 million in 2023). The Dragons have won five state titles (runners-up two other times) in the 21 years since. Not to be outdone, at least nine other suburban districts have built multi-million-dollar stadiums. Four facilities stood out above the rest during this spending spree: Cypress-Fairbanks ISD (2006, $80 million), Allen ISD (2012, $60 million), Katy ISD (2017, $70.3 million), and McKinney ISD (2018, $70 million). In each case the bonds contained funds for other athletic and academic facilities. For example, Allen built an indoor practice facility, a baseball/softball complex, and a strength & conditioning space that is better equipped than some in the NFL. There is even a golf-swing simulation room where student-athletes can have their swings captured for biomechanical video analysis.

All this money makes a significant impact on athletic performance. As in most states, Texas high schools are spilt into seven divisions based on student population, (6A-A and a separate six-man division). The top two divisions, 6A and 5A, are predominantly represented by urban and suburban districts in and around the five largest cities: Houston, which has Katy and Cypress-Fairbanks as suburbs, Dallas-Fort Worth (Allen, McKinney, and Southlake), Austin, and San Antonio. Since the relatively inexpensive Dragon Stadium opened in 2001, there have been 88 state titles contested in these top two divisions. Twenty-two of them (21.6%) have been won by schools that call one of these new stadiums home. When the 1013 independent school districts in Texas are ranked by average household income, 59 of the 88 state titles (69.3%) belong to schools from the top 20% in terms of income [5]. And this wealthy suburban dominance is not specific to football. Back to 2001, in addition to opening Dragon stadium, we opened a sparkling, new $7 million natatorium. That same year my boys' team won the state title and my girls' team finished second. Since then, the boys have won ten more titles, while the girls added another five trophies.

Like Texas high school athletics, American collegiate sports is dominated by football and to a lesser degree, men's basketball. In 1978 the NCAA split the top level of football playing schools, Division I, into two subdivisions based largely on the size of the respective student bodies and the seating capacity of each stadium. The larger schools, e.g., Alabama, Ohio State, etc. went into Division 1A (now called the Football Bowl Subdivision, FBS), while the smaller schools went into Division 1AA (now called the Football Championship Subdivision, FCS). Although each subdivision crowns its own national champion, most FBS schools will still schedule one FCS team to pad their record. In most cases, the FBS host school will pay for the privilege of playing their FCS guest. For example, during the 2022 football season, Alabama paid Austin Peay University (FCS) $600k to be their sacrificial lamb.

Until the early 1990s, FBS schools were largely assembled into regional athletic conferences, with a few independents here and there, e.g., Notre Dame. But over the last 30 years, a rapid infusion of money from ballooning television contracts has driven a mad reshuffling of programs as larger conferences poached the best remaining schools from their weaker neighbors. The ten FBS conferences have been split into two groups, the Power Five, which includes the Southeastern Conference (SEC), Big Ten (BIG10), Big Twelve (BIG12), PAC12, and the Atlantic Coastal Conference (ACC), and the Group of Five which includes the American Athletic Conference (AAC), Mountain West Conference (MWC), Sun Belt Conference (SunBelt), Mid-America Conference (MAC), and Conference USA (C-USA).

Having more TV exposure makes your alumni happy, and happy alumni (and envious, grumpy alumni) tend to donate more money (Table 1). In a desperate attempt to keep up with the Joneses, Group of Five schools have had to divert student fees away from what they really should be used for, i.e., academics, and use them to fund their football programs.

Table 1. Average donor contributions, media rights, student fees, and total coaches' salaries for all public FBS university football programs for the years 2014-2022, excluding the Covid-shortened 2020 season [6]. Money is in millions of dollars.

Conference	Average Payments to Coaches' Salaries	Donor Contributions	Media Rights,	Student Fees
Power Five				
SEC	$112.6	$272.0	$426.8	$2.2
BIG10	$97.2	$204.5	$395.9	$8.0
BIG12	$70.9	$216.7	$333.9	$8.6
ACC	$87.2	$206.1	$273.0	$62.0
PAC12	$77.9	$140.3	$263.8	$15.0
Group of Five				
AAC	$52.1	$67.3	$69.0	$85.0
MWC	$35.4	$52.8	$45.5	$33.0
C-USA	$25.2	$32.4	$27.0	$72.7
Sun Belt	$22.9	$19.6	$20.6	$44.4
MAC	$20.5	$16.8	$26.3	$84.2

The additional revenue allows Power Five schools to spend lavishly on athletic facilities that attract the country's best athletes, and by extension, the best non-athlete students, who want to attend schools with major, relevant football programs. Many of these students become successful, generous alumni who donate money to their alma maters at a scale and frequency that cannot be matched by Group of Five schools. But the biggest benefit of having more money is that it allows Power Five schools to pay the best coaches in the country and buy them out of their exorbitant contracts when they don't want them around anymore. For example, two years after signing their head coach, Jimbo Fisher to a 10-year contract extension, Texas A&M dumped him before the end of the 2023 season. His buyout? A cool $76 million. More money for salaries buys more wins. Excluding the COVID-shortened 2020 season, since the first year of the College Football Playoff (CFP) in 2014, the correlation between the total number of wins and total dollars spent on coaches' salaries

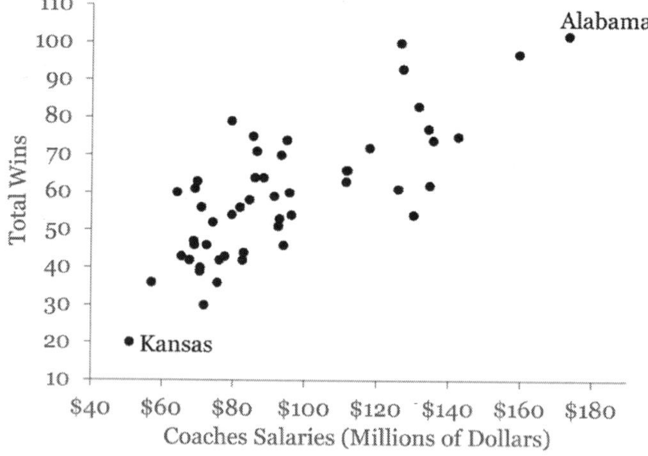

Figure 4. Total wins for all Power 5 football programs as a function of total money spent on coaches' salaries for the period 2014-2022, not including the Covid-shortened 2020 season.

among Power Five schools is 0.77, remember a perfect correlation is 1 (Figure 4).

Over this same period, the win-loss records for each SEC school (widely considered the best football conference) show the competitive advantage that comes with having more money (the highest average coaches' salaries). When playing against FCS opponents, the SEC went 123-2, winning 98.4% of the games (Vanderbilt and South Carolina take home the indignity as the only schools to eat losses). The average score of these games was 48-11. The Group of Five faired a little better, winning 12.6% of the time (220-29), with the average score of 38-16. It's not until we look at the SEC's record against their Power Five peers that we start to see some parity. When competing against the other four member conferences, the SEC went 109-100 (52.2%), winning by an average score of 29-26. If this isn't enough evidence for the inherent unfairness of the influence of money in amateur sports, the disparities become clearer still when we look at the results of the CFP.

Table 2. Total money spent on coaches' salaries for all public FBS university football programs that qualified for the CFP for the years 2014-2019 & 2021 [6]. Money is in millions of dollars. No data exists for either Notre Dame or TCU as they are private schools and do not have to report their finances publicly.

National Rank	School (Conference)	Coach Salary	CFP Appearances	Total CFP Championships
1	Alabama (SEC)	$173.2	8	3
2	Ohio State (BIG10)	$159.2	5	1
5	Louisiana State (SEC)	$142.4	1	1
6	Michigan (BIG10)	$134.2	3	1
7	Oklahoma (BIG12)	$131.4	4	0
8	Texas (BIG12)	$130.2	1	0
10	Georgia (SEC)	$127.0	3	2
11	Clemson (ACC)	$126.4	6	2
13	Michigan State (BIG10)	$111.7	1	0
14	Florida State (ACC)	$111.4	1	0
18	Oregon (PAC12)	$94.8	1	0
20	Washington (PAC12)	$93.2	2	0
No Data	TCU (BIG 12)	No Data	1	0
No Data	Notre Dame	No Data	2	0
50 (#1 Group of Five)	Cincinnati (AAC)	$62.6	1	0

Replacing the Bowl Championship Series, which pitted the top two teams against each other for the national championship at the end of each season, the CFP established a four-team, seeded bracket that provides two semi-final games, #1 vs. #4, and #2 vs. #3, followed by a national championship game. To date there have been ten iterations of the CFP. Of the 40 slots available, the SEC owns 12 selections (eight of those to Alabama), the BIG10 has nine (five to Ohio State), the ACC has seven (six to Clemson), the BIG12 has six (four to Oklahoma), the PAC12 has three, and Notre Dame has been selected twice. Only one team from the Group of Five has been selected, Cincinnati in 2021. Not surprisingly Cincinnati was the top ranked Group of Five team for coaches' salary. All that spending worked. Early in the 2021 season, it was announced that Cincinnati and three other Group of Five Schools, Houston, University of Central Florida (UCF), and Brigham Young University (BYU), had been invited to join the BIG12 and ascend to Power Five status. Like Cincinnati, Houston (#2) and UCF (#4) were highly ranked spenders in the Group of Five (no data is available for BYU since it is a private school). Just as in life, the rich get richer.

The take home message is that sports are anything but inherently fair because they are created by, and for, humans who are innately wired to be unfair. The negative impact that money has on sports far outweighs any potential threat posed by PED, and in my opinion is one of the biggest motivations to dope. Let me give you an example.

As I was putting the finishing touches on the last two chapters of this book in the summer of 2023, the PAC12 Conference was breaking apart. The dissolution of the second oldest major athletic conference in the country started a year earlier with the defections of its two most important members, the University of Southern California (USC) and their cross-town rival the University of California Los Angeles (UCLA) to the BIG10. The motivation to join a new conference whose closest school is over 1500 miles away from LA was solely driven by money, specifically TV revenue. The remaining ten schools stuck together until it became clear that there was more money to be made by jumping ship to another of the four remaining Power conferences. First Colorado declared that they were returning to their previous home, the BIG12. Then Oregon and Washington jumped ship to join USC and UCLA in the BIG10, but at a discounted rate. Both schools will only get half as much money as the other members, including USC and UCLA until a new TV deal is struck before the 2029-2030 academic year. That move prompted Arizona, Arizona State and Utah to move to the BIG12. Not to be left behind, Stanford and the University of California at Berkley (Cal) moved even further away and joined the ACC. That's right, two schools that are close enough to the Pacific Ocean that you can see it from their respective campuses now call the Atlantic Coast Conference home. Just like Oregon and Washington, Stanford and Cal are paying a hefty toll for their new places at the adult table. Each will receive only a 30% share of TV revenue for at least seven years. The price of admission. But the story doesn't end there. To even out the number of member schools at 18, the ACC also invited Southern Methodist University (SMU) in Dallas, Texas. SMU will receive no TV revenue, none, zip, for at least nine years. The gap in funding for each school will have to be made up by donations from wealthy donors who are all too happy to finally be a member of a Power conference.

Because of all these desperate moves by already wealthy schools to ensure their place at the trough, student athletes from Sandford and Cal will now regularly have to travel thousands of miles, as far away as Syracuse, New York and Boston, Massachusetts to compete in every sport, not just football. How is this what's best for their student-athletes? How does this accomplish the academic mission of any institution of higher learning? Of course, it doesn't. But who cares about educating our next generation when you can pay your football coaches, athletics directors, chancellors, and presidents more money? Conspicuously absent from this list of beneficiaries are the people who we actually tune in to watch on TV, the student-athletes, and by that, I mean the football and men's basketball teams. No disrespect to female collegiate athletes, but relatively few people watch women's basketball, and almost no one watches the other collegiate Olympic sports. In 2019, while the men's basketball tournament was busy clearing $917.8 million, the women's basketball tournament operated at a loss of $2.8 million [7].

Even though college football and men's basketball generate billions of dollars for the NCAA and its member institutions each year, the young men who risk serious injury every time they lace up their sneakers get nothing from their universities but a diploma that is often not worth the paper it's written on, and that's assuming they graduate. A joint study conducted by the National Collegiate Players Association (NCPA) and Drexel University in 2011 estimated that 86% of players on full scholarship were forced to live below the federal poverty line [8]. That's right, while your head coach is making millions in salary and endorsement deals, you get to live off a steady diet of Ramen noodles and spaghetti. Thankfully, after decades of making their labor force work for free, a unanimous decision by the Supreme Court in June 2021 compelled the NCAA to allow college athletes to be paid for the use of their names, images, and likenesses (NIL). Student-athletes can now make money from endorsement deals just like the pros.

Make no mistake, NIL is a good thing. But this model has a major flaw. While the most talented and marketable athletes are generating NIL money, the rest of the team is still living below the poverty line. What greater motivation to do whatever you must to get paid? Can anyone really claim surprise when they hear a news story about a group of college football players from Money Maker University who succumbed to the temptations of doping to enhance their athletic performance under these circumstances? All the adults who run the show have modelled nothing but greedy, reckless behavior for decades, destroying regional rivalries, increasing travel and time away from the classroom, and commodifying the young men and women they are supposed to be guiding into adulthood, all the while acquiring generational wealth for themselves, or at least trying to. What would you do if you were on the second team and you thought a little boost would be the difference between making a little extra money and another semester of bologna sandwiches? What would I have done when I was 18-22? *"Hey coach, you got yours, I'm about to get mine."*

I am not advocating for anyone to take PED that may have serious adverse effects on their health. But there is an argument to be made that playing football is at least as dangerous as taking many PED, if not more so. These young men risk their health, and potentially their lives, every time they run out on to the field to smash themselves into other young men for our viewing pleasure. You don't have to agree with anyone's decision to take PED. But I think empathy is a pre-requisite to judging anyone for doing what they see their leaders do every day: win at just about any cost.

Reference:

1. O'Neill, A. *Number of athletes at the Summer Olympics by gender 1896-2020*. 2023; Available from: https://www.statista.com/statistics/1090581/olympics-number-athletes-by-gender-since-1896/.
2. Bank, W. *List of Countries by GDP (2020)*. 2021; Available from: https://statisticstimes.com/economy/countries-by-gdp.php.
3. Heming, T. *Why is There a Lack of Diversity in Triathlon?* 220 Triathlon, 2020.
4. Expert, Z.T.C. *Swimmer Demographics and Statistics in the U.S*. 2021; Available from: https://www.zippia.com/swimmer-jobs/demographics/.

5. McCann, A. *Most & Least Equitable School Districts in Texas*. 2023; Available from: https://wallethub.com/edu/e/most-least-equitable-school-districts-in-texas/77134.
6. Athletics, K.C.o.I. *Knight-Newhouse College Athletics Database*. 2005-2023; Available from: https://knightnewhousedata.org/.
7. Emily Caron, E.N.-W. *March Madness Daily: The NCAA's Undervalued Women'sTV Rrights*. Sportico: The Business of Sports, 2021.
8. Huma, R. *The Price of Poverty in Big Time College Sport*. 2011.

Chapter 3. Pan y Agua

*"Two things scare me. The first is getting hurt. But that's not nearly as scary as the second, which is losing."— **Lance Armstrong***

On the afternoon of July 13, 1999, I was rivetted to my couch, watching Lance Armstrong raise his hands above his head, casting his eyes to the rain-soaked sky after winning the 9th stage of the Tour de France on the summit of the Col de Sestriere. Having no history as a strong climber, Armstrong was expected to lose the Yellow jersey worn by the overall race leader as the race entered the Alps. Instead, he dominated the stage, leapfrogging between small groups of the World's best climbers. As he closed in on the two leaders of the day's stage, the Italian Ivan Gotti and Spaniard Fernando Escartin, a moment of disbelief registered on both of their faces as they each did a noticeable double take when they realized that it was Armstrong who had joined them. Armstrong rode effortlessly, his upper body still and calm, his cadence fast and smooth. His face expressed concentration, but no hint of a grimace or sneer. By contrast Escartin and Gotti were clearly laboring. Their shoulders were hunched as they both rocked side to side, standing up, out of their saddles, stomping on their pedals in slower, uneven rhythms. Armstrong started the day with a lead of 2:20 in the general classification (GC) and finished with an advantage of 6:43. When he crossed the finish line in Paris on July 25th, his final margin of victory was 7:37. For all intents and purposes, Armstrong won the race that day in the Italian Alps.

Almost immediately I began to hear the skeptics questioning the legitimacy of Armstrong's performance. After all, this was only one year removed from the Festina scandal that almost caused the cancellation of the 1998 Tour. On July 8th of that year, Willy Voet, a soigneur for the top ranked Festina cycling team was pulled over by French police at the

Belgian border with a doper's cornucopia in the trunk of his team-owned car. According to Voet in his book, *Breaking the Chain, Drugs and Cycling*, he was transporting 234 vials of Erythropoietin (EPO), 80 flasks of human growth hormone (HGH), 160 capsules of testosterone, 60 pills of blood thinners (to prevent blood clots in their EPO-thickened blood), and a large quantity of amphetamines, syringes, and needles [1]. Of the 189 cyclists who started the race, only 96 finished, with most of the attrition resulting from riders either being kicked out of the race or quitting to avoid police interrogations that allegedly involved body cavity searches.

The 1999 Tour was supposed to be the *"Tour of Renewal,"* a clean race, purged of all doping, raced on "*pan y agua*," or only on bread and water, a euphemistic inside joke about the prevalence of doping in the peloton. But how on Earth had Lance Armstrong, an abrasive Texan, who in four tries had only completed the race once, finishing 36th, won the Super Bowl of cycling? Skepticism was a natural response. When you add to this the fact that he was just three years removed from a diagnosis of stage four testicular cancer, the result was truly unbelievable. As reasonable as these questions were, the race organizers, television networks, corporate sponsors, and most importantly, the fans, wouldn't, or couldn't listen to the doubters. The story was just too good. Instead of his dance with death being a source of suspicion, it was the foundation of the greatest inspirational, feel-good, comeback story of a generation. Armstrong was exactly what the Tour de France, and to a greater extent, the entire sport of cycling desperately needed. That seven-year stretch between 1999 and 2005, when Armstrong won a record seven consecutive Tours de France, saw both the Tour and the sport of cycling rapidly increase in popularity. Every ship in the cycling sea was lifted to unimaginable heights. Quite simply, Armstrong saved the Tour de France from relegation into the realm of niche sports like boxing and horse racing and helped grow cycling into a money-making juggernaut. This fact created an inherent motivation to look the other way and keep the money spigot flowing.

I was as guilty as anyone, suspending my better judgement and common sense and choosing to believe the unbelievable. Having won my own battle with testicular cancer in 1999 at 24 years old, I was a big Lance Armstrong fan. I appreciated his cockiness and his tactical awareness on the bike. Armstrong could switch between a cagy counterpuncher and a brawler depending on what the situation required. But the best way to describe Armstrong was that he was a bully. It wasn't so much that I didn't want to believe that Armstrong was doping as it was that I just assumed that when an athlete passed a doping control test it meant he or she was clean. For the record, Armstrong has never failed a doping control test at the time it was administered. I'll clarify this point later.

Shortly after the conclusion of the 1999 Tour I bought a poster of Armstrong crossing the finish line at Sestriere. I needed some wall art for my new apartment. A few days later I moved from my hometown of Houston to College Station, Texas to start my master's degree in exercise physiology at Texas A&M. It was during this time that I began to gain a better understanding of the incredible physical toll a three-week stage race takes on the body. But instead of giving me any pause for concern, it just provided justification to make their pedestals a little taller.

Over the next six years my plans for the month of July revolved around the daily broadcasts of the Tour. In 2003 I took a trip to Europe with my sister, making two stops to watch stage finishes, in Bordeaux and Paris. This was the only one of his victories when Armstrong was meaningfully challenged, beating the 1997 winner, Germany's Jan Ullrich, by just 1:01. The 2003 win also pulled him level with four other legendary cyclists as the only men to win the Tour five times:

- France's Jacque Anquetil (1957 and 1961-1964), the incestuous love triangle guy and an unabashed doper rode in the era before doping was banned in 1965 [2].
- Arguably the greatest cyclist of all time, Belgian, Eddy Merckx (1969-1972 and 1974) tested positive for stimulants on at least three occasions during his career, the first led to his disqualification while wearing the leader's pink jersey during the 1969 Giro d'Italia [3].
- The last Frenchman to win the Tour, and commonly considered the second-best rider in history, Bernard Hinault, (1978-1979, 1981-1982, and 1985). Although he never failed a doping control test, he did skip one after the Critérium de Callac in 1982, which is punished the same as failing a test [4].
- Finally, the only person to win the Tour five consecutive times, Spaniard Miguel Indurain, (1991-1995). Technically, Indurain never tested positive, but he was caught using the asthma medication Salbutomal in 1994 [4]. He avoided suspension because Salbutomal was an approved treatment for athletes with respiratory problems. That said, Indurain dominated the world of cycling during a time when EPO was changing the sport. Indeed, all eight of the men who finished either second or third to Indurain during his five-year reign as Tour de France champion either failed doping controls, were implicated in doping schemes, or admitted to doping at some point.

After returning home from my trip to Europe I began my doctoral studies in exercise physiology at the University of Houston. It was during this time that I began to learn more about the history of doping and how prevalent the practice was, and still is, in many sports. But still, I kept following every second of coverage, cheering my fellow Texan on to his record-breaking sixth victory in 2004. But it was the first stage of the 2005 Tour that planted the first seeds of doubt in my head. Two years of doctoral work had begun to change me from an eternal optimist to a hardened skeptic. The Tour typically begins with a prologue, or short time trial, during which the riders are set off one at a time between one and three minutes apart. Each athlete must ride alone against the clock. If they are caught by, or overtake another rider, the two cannot ride together to gain an advantage over the rest of the field. This is why the time trial is called, *"the race of truth."* It's just you versus the clock.

The prologue of the 2005 Tour was a quick 11.8-mile jaunt, a distance that should have been too short for any of the GC contenders to gain any more than a few seconds advantage on anyone else. Riders are set off in reverse order with the slower riders going first and the faster/higher placed riders going later. If there is a defending champion, he goes last on the day. On this day, Armstrong started last, and Jan Ullrich left the start house a minute before him. The contrast of their styles was stark. Armstrong pushed a smaller gear and relied on a faster cadence to generate his speed, while Ullrich pedaled more slowly in a much bigger gear. Although it looked like Armstrong was having a better day, I was stunned to see him catch and pass Ullrich with less than a mile to go. In my extensive experience of watching cycling, I had never seen such a dominant performance over such a short distance. The final margin was 1:06, a huge chunk of time to concede on the first day of a 2000+ mile race. Make no mistake, Jan Ullrich was no chump. He had won the Tour in 1997 and finished second on five other occasions, three of them behind Armstrong. There was no way that Armstrong should have been able to beat Ullrich by more than a minute in less than 12 miles. Something didn't add up, but I wasn't exactly sure what was wrong with the equation. Three weeks later, Armstrong retired after winning his seventh consecutive Tour de France title and the scramble to fill the void left after his departure began.

As is usually the case with a massive coverup, the eventual deluge of damaging information is preceded by a slow, but persistent drip, drip, drip of leaks. For me, the first drip was the 2005 prologue. The next droplets came in rapid, dramatic succession over the course of the next year. On May 6th, 2006, Spanish Civil Police raided properties belonging to Eufemiano Fuentes, the team doctor for the Spanish team, Kelme, in an anti-doping sting code-named *Operación Puerto* (Operation Mountain Pass). In addition to the expected trove of doping products including testosterone and 100 bags of blood belonging to several cyclists, they also found a coded list including several names of elite cyclists who had paid Fuentes for his doping services [5]. At the top of the list were Ivan Basso (2nd place 2005) and Ullrich. Basso and Ullrich sought cover and dropped out of the 2006 Tour, leaving it wide open for a new champion to take the top step on the podium in Paris. Enter American Floyd Landis, a former Armstrong teammate who served as his top lieutenant during the 2004 Tour.

The 2006 race saw one of the most dramatic 24-hour turnarounds that I have ever seen in any sporting event. By stage 16, Landis was in the Yellow jersey, holding a scant 10 second lead over Spaniard Oscar Pereiro. The day's stage took the peloton over four massive alpine summits including the storied Col du Galibier. Landis had a terrible day in the saddle, losing an unbelievable 8:18 to Pereiro and dropping to 11th place. Prior to stage 17, with nothing to lose, Landis and his team decided that they needed to go on an all-out attack when the race approached the first climb of the day. Word of the impending assault spread through the peloton.

> *"Somehow, word got out around the peloton that we were going to do that (go to the front on the first climb) and people came up to*

me saying I was crazy, please don't do it... I told 'em, please go drink some Coke because we're leaving on the first climb if you want to come with us." ***Floyd Landis***

Landis rode at the front of the race for almost 60 miles that day, destroying the field, and moving back up to 3rd place, only 30 seconds behind Pereiro. Landis would take over the lead for good after the stage 19 time trial, winning his first Yellow jersey by 57 seconds. Unfortunately, a few days after the finish of the Tour, it was revealed that Landis had failed his doping control test after stage 17, his remarkable recovery was attributed to synthetic testosterone, and *not* Coca-cola. He was disqualified and given a two-year ban. Having been a Floyd fan, I was bitterly disappointed with the outcome. But, unlike most fans, my anger wasn't only aimed at Landis. I was now certain that Lance Armstrong had cheated throughout his seven-year miracle comeback.

Over the course of three months, it had been revealed that two of Lance's toughest rivals, Basso and Ullrich, and two of his former teammates-turned rivals had cheated. Another prominent name on the Fuentes list was Tyler Hamilton, who had ridden for Armstrong for his first three wins from 1999-2001 [5]. Hamilton left to lead his own team in 2002 and finished 4th in the 2003 Tour. Over the coming months, as more names from *Operación Puerto* were leaked, or as athletes failed more doping controls, I started to catalog the names of the men who had finished on the podium with Armstrong over his seven-year run. Like what happened from 1991-1995 with Miguel Indurain, of the eight men who finished either 2nd or 3rd to Armstrong, only one, Fernando Escartin has never been associated with doping during his career. In preparing to write this book, I extended my analysis to the top ten finishers from 1999-2005. Of the 36 men who finished 2nd – 10th to Armstrong, only nine have never had their names tarnished by doping allegations. That's 75% of the top 10 riders over seven years who are known to have cheated. I suspect that this is a conservative number. In the most jaded view, this only means that the other nine men didn't get caught.

What I was left with was the harsh reality of a binary outcome. Either Lance Armstrong, a cyclist who prior to 1999 was a mediocre climber at best, a man who had survived a disease that required weeks of harsh chemotherapy and brain surgery to remove several tumors, had come all the way back on *pan y agua* to absolutely dominate the world's toughest athletic event seven times, beating the tar out of a peloton filled with confirmed dopers, or he had leveled the playing field and doped as well. Logically, the only answer that made sense was the latter. For it to be the former, Armstrong would have to be a physiological marvel, the likes of which the world had literally never seen before or since. There was published data that showed otherwise. In terms of aerobic capacity, Armstrong was not one of the most gifted cyclists on the planet [6].

In the fall of 2007, I came across a book written by a sportswriter-turned investigative journalist named David Walsh, called *From Lance to Landis* [7]. The case against Armstrong being a clean rider was made clearly and objectively. It turned out that he actually had failed one doping control during the 1999 Tour, for cortisone, a commonly used doping agent. Armstrong and his team scrambled to find a topical cream that contained the exact form of cortisone that he had illegally injected. The team doctor backdated a prescription for the cream, claiming that it was used to treat a saddle sore. The race organizers lamely accepted this pathetic excuse for a legitimate use of an otherwise banned substance and kept the gravy train rolling. More damning still was the revelation that when the frozen urine samples from 1999 Tour were retrospectively analyzed for EPO in 2005 using a series of new tests, at least eight of

Armstrong's samples came back positive for the blood boosting hormone.

As more evidence of Lance's cheating came out, he did what most people with power and influence do when they are desperately trying to keep a secret, he bullied everyone who had something to say. This is an abridged list of the people whom Lance Armstrong went after.

- In 2004, Emma O'Reilly, the former soigneur for the US Postal Service team who worked for Armstrong from 1996-2000, gave an interview to David Walsh for his book, *LA Confidential,* in which she revealed that she had used makeup to cover up bruises from needle marks, and had disposed of materials that she correctly assumed to be doping products [8]. Armstrong responded by calling O'Reilly an alcoholic and a prostitute, in a successful campaign to sully her name.
- Armstrong sued David Walsh and his employer, the *Sunday Times of London* for libel in 2004 after it printed a story that suggested he had doped during his winning run in the Tour de France. The case was settled in 2006, after the *Sunday Times* relented and issued an apology. Of course, this only galvanized his supporters to believe that he was clean, and why not? He did what we expect of anyone who is telling the truth while being called a liar, he sued and won.
- Finally, there was the case of Filippo Simeoni. He had also doped with the assistance of Michele Ferrari, the disgraced Italian sports doctor who had directed Armstrong's doping. After serving a doping suspension and testifying against Ferrari in a criminal case in the Italian courts, Simeoni returned to competition. Armstrong made it publicly known that he considered Simeoni a snitch and didn't approve of him testifying against his doping mentor. To the

contrary, Armstrong expected Simeoni to follow the cycling code of silence, or the *omerta*, an Italian term most often associated with the Mafia. This came to a head at the end of the 2004 Tour. When Simeoni tried to join an early breakaway, Armstrong, wearing the yellow jersey, chased down the lead group and told everyone present that he would stay with them until Simeoni fell back to the main group. This meant that the rest of the peloton would be obliged to chase down Armstrong and the breakaway, and none of these second and third tier riders would have a chance at a stage win. Unsurprisingly, the other members of the breakaway implored Simeoni to return to peloton while they carried on. Looking defeated, Simeoni reluctantly dropped back with Armstrong to join the peloton. Wearing a Cheshire grin, Armstrong looked directly into the camera, and mockingly drew his pinched fingers across his pursed lips, as if to say, *"I can make anyone zip their mouths shut."*

As much as I like confidence in my sporting heroes, this went well beyond gamesmanship. For me, Armstrong's behavior on this day was, at best, unsportsmanlike. At worst, he looked like a crime boss threatening to knee-cap a guy if he didn't shut his mouth. While watching this scene play out on TV, I remember asking myself,

"Why would you do this? Why give your haters even more ammunition to use against you? This makes you look guilty, Lance! Why would you act like someone actively silencing a witness, ON LIVE TELEVISION NO LESS?!"

Later that day, I took down my poster of Armstrong winning the Sestriere stage in 1999 and tossed it in the trash. Although this was a year before the prologue of the 2005 Tour when he beat a doped Ulrich by more than a minute, his behavior that day made him unworthy of a place on my wall.

Had Armstrong stayed retired it is likely that he would have avoided the most damaging parts of his eventual downfall, including losing over $100 million in sponsorship contracts, becoming *persona non grata* to the Livestrong Foundation that he founded, being sued by the federal government in a civil corruption trial that was eventually settled for $5 million, and being given a lifetime ban from competing in any event sanctioned by any sport governing body associated with either the United States Anti-Doping Agency (USADA) or the World Anti-Doping Agency (WADA). The ban includes events as big as the Boston Marathon, and those as small as local sprint triathlons and 5k's. Not a small punishment for a life-long athlete.

But, in a show of pure hubris, Armstrong chose to come back and compete in the 2009 and 2010 Tours. His return to the sport while cycling was undergoing a purification process, purging as many dopers as it could find, was the last proverbial straw. The governing body of cycling, the Union Cycliste Internationale (UCI), USADA and WADA all wanted Armstrong gone. Here is where the analogy of Lance Armstrong as a crime boss comes to its logical and inevitable conclusion. How do you take down a Mafia boss? You find a former associate who knows where the blood bags are hanging and offer him a deal. Then you go after as many of the boss' underlings as you can to gather evidence against the boss. Re-enter Floyd Landis for his second act.

After Landis served his two-year suspension for doping during the 2006 Tour, he wanted back in the game. He asked Lance for help. Understandably, he didn't get what he had asked for. At this point, Landis was radioactive and had Armstrong given him a spot on his new team for the 2009 season, he would have put an even larger target on his back than was already present. Landis responded by turning state's evidence and filing a whistleblower civil case against Armstrong, as part of the larger federal case. Landis was eventually awarded $1 million in the settlement. Landis also fingered several of his former teammates who, after being promised lighter punishments, gave their own sworn testimonies implicating Armstrong as the mastermind of the doping plot. Knowing that USADA was going to release a 202-page report detailing the workings of the Lance Armstrong doping machine [9], Armstrong agreed to a tell-all interview with Oprah Winfrey that was televised over two nights on January 17th & 18th, 2013. Defiant to the end, this was Armstrong's final effort to control the narrative of his demise.

Between the time of the Simeoni affair in 2004 and the release of the USADA report in June 2012, my feelings about Armstrong had evolved from that of a wary supporter to an angry detractor. Although I was disappointed by the doping, what infuriated me was how Armstrong had continued to brutalize anyone who spoke out against him. There was never an ounce of nuance to his response. It was always a full-on attack against anyone and everyone who questioned the legitimacy of his reign. This led to several heated conversations with my friends in the cycling and triathlon communities, academic colleagues, and even with a few of my students. Unlike these good people, I knew how easy it was to evade detection while doping. But getting people to believe that Lance Armstrong was a drug cheat was nearly impossible. Most people had too much emotionally invested in their hero-worship.

I spent the days before the airing of the Oprah interview gloating. I posted an *"I told you so"* message on my Facebook page that started several conversations, mostly jovial, but there were contributions that were raw and angry. It felt good to be vindicated in such black and white terms. I was right! Lance Armstrong was a drug cheat, a doper, and now everyone was going to know it. But my celebratory feelings of self-righteous indignation and anger quickly faded when the interview began. For the first time ever, I saw Lance Armstrong humbled, and I liked the new version of him. By the end of the interview, I was at peace with what Armstrong had done. He provided a public *mea culpa* and had begun the process of apologizing to many of the people he had harmed during his self-defense. In my view, the rest of that process was between Armstrong and those whom he had attacked. I knew he was going to pay a huge price for his misdeeds: the loss of millions in sponsorships, and millions more in legal fees and penalties. More importantly, he would be trading in his role as national hero for that of pariah. To be sure, Armstrong deserved his punishment. But once it was done, in my opinion, he was square with the house.

After the Oprah interview, I stopped paying attention to cycling. I read about subsequent doping scandals when they happened, each of which provided further evidence for my jaded opinion that the entire sport was tainted and a waste of my time. Although this left a void, I was busy with career and family. Fast forward to the spring of 2020. Like many academics, the Covid pandemic had me stuck at home, teaching remotely. During a break between classes, I was watching old sporting events on YouTube when I happened across a broadcast of the 1987 Tour on CBS. Unlike today, when each stage of the tour is broadcast live, from start to finish, with continuous commentary about every acceleration, and periodic history lessons about each cathedral, chapel, and châteaux along the route, the early American broadcasts were one to two-hour summaries of the previous week's highlights. The events of each stage would be spliced together over a quintessentially 80's techno soundtrack. They were less sports broadcast than they were well-produced TV dramas, loosely following an obscure sporting event that most Americans knew nothing about.

To dramatize the agony that accompanies hauling exhausted bodies over the Alps and Pyrenees on bicycles, the producers added several super-slow-motion segments of tormented cyclists, mouths agape, eyes squinting, drool hanging from their chins, slowly, agonizingly turning over their pedals as they ascended to brutally steep heights. If you watch it yourself, skip to the second hour. The coverage opens with a montage of carnage. One poor soul is airlifted on a backboard. Another is shown riding with blood streaming down his face. You can even see the eventual winner, Stephen Roache, being loaded into an ambulance after collapsing at the end of stage 21. I remember thinking to myself: *"It's no wonder why these poor bastards take drugs, they're all beat to hell for three straight weeks."*

Beyond the spectacle that was the 1987 Tour, something I'll talk about at length in Chapter 4, what struck me most about the broadcast was how the scripted narration painted a bleak picture of the Tour de France as a torturous event that its competitors were lucky to survive. Before writing this chapter, I went back and catalogued the words used to describe the struggle to finish the Tour in one piece. Over a little more than two hours, the word, *"attack"* was used 16 times, while synonyms of *"suffering"* and *"pain"* were each used eight times. I also took note of several excellent quotes that hammered home the intended point of emphasis that this race was not your typical sporting event with high fives and celebration dances. It was more like a scene from a triage hospital in a medical drama.

A critical stage in that year's race was a mountain time trial up the legendary Mont Ventoux, on whose slopes in 1967 English cyclist Tom Simpson died of heat exhaustion, likely exacerbated by amphetamines and brandy. In a prelude to the stage, the commentator, a former amateur cyclist, Phil Ligget said,

> *"For 171 young men it will be this mountain where they came willingly to pay perhaps the final price for their quest."*

The FINAL price!? What the hell does that mean? Were they expecting fatalities?

It was clear that CBS sports, and the Tour de France, knew exactly what they were doing. Sports are a metaphor for life, and humans recognize and respect the struggle to overcome. It makes for great television. Just look back to the introduction for ABC's "Wide World of Sports." Sportscaster Jim McCay narrated.

"Spanning the globe to bring you the constant variety of sport.
The thrill of victory, and the agony of defeat.
The human drama of athletic competition.
This is ABC's Wide World of Sports."

The agony of defeat is personified by Yugoslavian ski jumper Vinko Bogataj careening down the ramp at the World Championships in Obersdorf, Germany in 1970. As he approached his take off point, snow flurries and gusting winds threw off his balance as he desperately attempted to stop his approach. Instead, Bogataj went spinning sideways off the side of the ramp, slamming backward into the ground twenty feet below. That footage was shown weekly, most Saturday afternoons from 1971 to 1998. Why? Because carnage, or at least the potential of serious injury, sells. That was the hook to keep people watching. If they only showed happy people crossing the finish line unscathed, no one would watch, advertisers would stay away, and the network wouldn't make any money. This is particularly true for cycling. Watching people riding bikes during a flat stage is really, really boring. But as soon as someone attacks while descending a narrow mountain pass at 60+ mph, without a helmet, and in driving rain or snow, well that's entertaining!

Beyond the graphic language and images of trauma, one short, eight second story blew my mind. Phil Ligget was setting up the finish of stage 6, a flat course typically contested by cyclists with supporting roles, and not the GC contenders. On this day it came down to two men, Mexican Raul Alcala, and Frenchman Christophe Lavainne, with the stage winner having a good chance of grabbing the Yellow jersey for a few days before the race entered the mountains where the true champion would be decided. As sportscasters often do, Ligget was providing context to the race by telling the audience some interesting facts about each man. There was plenty to say about Alcala. He was the first Mexican to compete in the Tour and he rode for the upstart, American 7-Eleven team. But Lavainne, who would win the stage, was a lesser-known commodity. That's when Ligget dropped this nugget of knowledge.

> *"His [Alcala's] main rival for the leader's Yellow jersey is young Frenchman Christophe Lavainne, forced to become a pro early because his parents couldn't afford to keep him at home."*

I had to back the video up to be sure that I heard him correctly. Lavainne's parents were so poor that they couldn't afford to feed him anymore, and if he wanted to eat, he had to either turn to manual labor or become a professional one or two years before most cyclists would be considered ready. Now, that's not to say that there is anything wrong with manual labor. I've certainly done my share. But if given the choice, I'd pick sports over working in the fields or a factory. That one sentence provided perspective about the choices that many of these cyclists faced in the 1980s and 1990s. This was particularly true after the dissolution of the Iron Curtain, when the relatively lucrative world of professional cycling was finally opened to Eastern Bloc riders from comparatively poorer countries.

I thought about Christophe Lavainne the rest of the day. Actually, I didn't think about him so much as I did his circumstance. How many other cyclists were, and still are, faced with that choice? By the same token, how many

American football, baseball, and basketball players from inner city or rural communities hope to use their athletic talents as their only ticket out of generational poverty? How many more wish they could, but lack the talent, or get injured before they can take advantage of their skills? After wrapping up my work for the day, I put these thoughts out of my head and sat down to watch some TV when serendipity struck. There was an advertisement for the ESPN documentary series, "30 for 30." The next episode was a two-parter titled *LANCE*. Ain't life strange?

As compelling as his interview with Oprah was, *LANCE* was brilliant, compelling storytelling. As biographies should be, it was a balanced, thorough account of his life and career, including his doping, and just as importantly, his bullying cover-up. I believed his explanation for why he started doping. By the mid 1990s he found himself faced with a stark decision, either join the doping arms race or quit and go home. It was that simple. Professional cycling teams are paid for with sponsorships from corporations who want their logos riding at the front of the peloton on a regular basis. If you don't get yourself on the podium as a walking, talking, breathing billboard, you are of no use to your sponsors. It's a business. Produce or go home.

I was surprised to find myself empathizing with Armstrong. Beyond the fact that he had only a high school education and no real job skills, he was a fierce competitor whose entire existence revolved around being a professional cyclist. The choice to dope, or not dope, was just another challenge issued by his rivals. *"Are you man enough to do what is necessary to compete?"* I wondered what I would do if I grew up in similar circumstances; the product of a broken family who didn't know his father, he was raised by his mother until she remarried a man who, by all accounts was a strict disciplinarian who often resorted to the belt. I asked myself what I would do if the difference between becoming a professional athlete or remaining in poverty came down to whether or not I would take performance enhancing drugs (PED). I have no doubt, between the ages of 18-35, I would have taken anything offered to me if it would allow me to provide for my family, maintain my identity, and most importantly, if it would level the playing field.

But that brings up an interesting point. For Armstrong to have leveled the playing field, someone else in another time had to be the first to tip the scales to their advantage. What was the motivation of the first cyclist to turn to doping? Considering just how brutal the first iterations of the Tour were, I suspect that doping was a direct response to the pain and suffering that the Tour organizer, Henri Desgragné, conceived. The first Tour de France in 1903 covered 1509 miles over just six stages on gravel roads and goat tracks. On average, each stage covered 250 miles with the longest being the last stage from Nantes to Paris at 293 miles. The bikes were fixed gear tanks weighing in at 35-45 lbs. and made of relatively low-quality steel that would frequently crack from the jarring impacts of the poor roads.

Then seven years later, to add to the suffering and satisfy the fans, Desgrangè started sending the riders over the mountains. During the 10th stage of the 1910 Tour, the riders went over four of the toughest mountains in all of cycling: The Peyresourde, Aspin, Tourmalet, and Aubisque. Indeed, so awful was the 202-mile stage that the eventual winner, Frenchman Octave Lapize, was forced to dismount his bike on the Aubisque and walk it the last several miles to the summit. When he arrived as the peak, he was so angered by the difficulty of the course that he screamed at the race organizers. *"Vous êtes des assassins!" [You are assassins!][10].* This is a pattern that would repeat throughout the history of the Tour until today. The race organizers think the race needs a jolt to make it more exciting for the fans. More excited fans spend more on merchandise and watch TV broadcasts that generate more advertising revenue. But the harder the race became, the more PED the athletes took to survive. Whoever suffers the least or the most efficiently wins the day.

Reference:

1. Voet, W., *Breaking the Chain: Drugs and Cycling, The True Story*. 2001, London, England, UK: Yellow Jersey Press.
2. Howard, P., *Sex, Lies, and Handlebar Tape: The Remarkable Life of Jacques Anquetil, The First Five-Times Winner of the Tour de France*. 2011, Edinburgh, Scotland, UK: Mainstream Publishing Company.
3. Friebe, D., *Eddy Merckx: The Cannibal*. 2012, London, England, UK: Ebury Press.
4. *Dopeology*. Available from: https://www.dopeology.org/people/Bernard_Hinault/.
5. Coyle, T.H.D., *The Secret Race: Inside the Hidden World of the Tour de France, Doping, Cover Ups, and Winning at All Costs*. 2012, New York, New York, USA: Bantam Books.
6. Edward F. Coyle, P., *Lance Armstrong's Physiological Maturation*. 2005.
7. Walsh, D., *From Lance to Landis*. 2007, New York, New York, USA: Balantine Book.
8. Walsh, P.B.D., *L.A. Confidentiel: Les Secrets de Lance Armstrong*. 2004, Paris, France: La Martinière.
9. (USADA), U.S.A.-D.A., *Reasoned Decision of the United States Anti-Doping Agency on Disqualification and Ineligibility*. 2012.
10. McGann, B.C., *The Story of the Tour de France*. Vol. 1: 1903-1975. 2019, McMinnville, Oregon, USA: McGann Publishing.

Chapter 4: What doesn't kill you...

"Everything is okay, mais pas de femme ce soir." Translation... but no women this evening.
– Stephen Roche 1987 Tour de France Champion

The 1999 Tour de France was dubbed the *"Race of Renewal"* by its organizers, in a desperate attempt to distance itself from the Festina Affair of the prior year. Of course, the central figure in 1999 was Lance Armstrong, returning from a near fatal battle with testicular cancer that took him away from racing for the better part of two seasons between 1996-1998. The perceived ease of Armstrong's relatively large margin of victory, 7:37, immediately aroused suspicions. Namely, Irish sports journalist David Walsh, who was instrumental in bringing down Armstrong and other prominent cyclists of the era. In his initial argument Walsh cited the fact that instead of getting slower, in what was supposed to be a new era of road cycling liberated from the shackles of doping, the average speed for the entire field, and Armstrong specifically, was actually the fastest in the history of the race to that point.

But comparing race speeds from year to year is not a good measure of athletic performance or the difficulty of the race route. Because of this, average speed is a poor predictor for the presence or absence of performance enhancing drugs (PED). Race speed is influenced by several factors including team tactics, weather conditions, and technological advancements in training, recovery, nutrition, and equipment, and finally, the distance of the race itself. For example, although the average speed of the field in 1999 was faster than during the 1998 Tour (41.43 km/h vs. 41.08 km/h), it was also a slightly shorter course (3870 km vs. 3875 km), with much better weather conditions, and no late-night raids of team hotel rooms, or hours-long police interrogations. If we look at the relationship between the average speed of the field and the distance of the race over the entire history of the Tour de France (Figure 5), there is a clear inverse relationship, as the Tour has gotten progressively faster over the years, it has also gotten shorter.

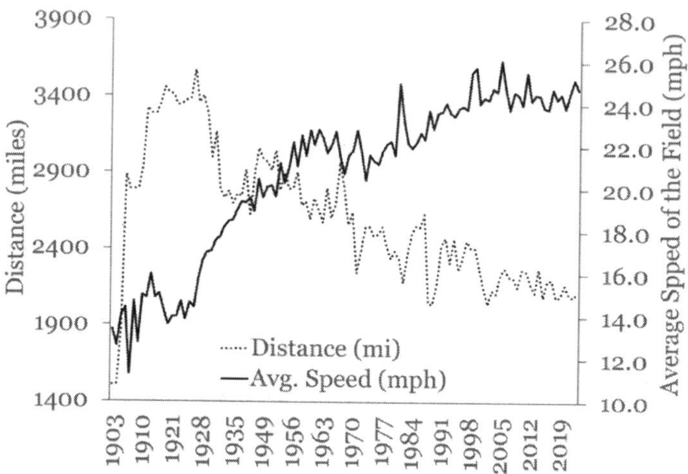

Figure 5. Although it is likely that PED played a role in the increase in average speed for the Tour de France over the years, there are many other factors at play including the distance of the race which has progressively decreased since its peak in 1926.

That said, there was a well-publicized effort on the part of the Tour organizers, Amaury Sport Organisation (ASO) to make the races of the early 2000s less harrowing than those of the 1990s, when doping reached its peak. The motivation to deter doping by reducing the perceived need for PED raises the obvious question: is there evidence in the historical record of the Tour de France that shows a connection between the difficulty of the race route and the introduction of new doping products and methods in the Peloton?

Answering this question required an objective measure of race difficulty. For this new measure I turned to the part of the Tour de France that makes it an interesting spectator sport, the mountains. When analyzing television viewership in ten European countries including France, Germany, and Italy, during the 2019 Tour de France, mountain stages drew 49% more viewers than did the flat stages [1]. Time trial stages were the least watched, drawing 8% fewer viewers than flat stages. If you've ever watched the Tour de France, this data makes sense. When compared to the mountain stages, flat stages are boring. In most instances, the Peloton sticks together in a fast-moving mass of two-wheeled humanity. Most of the drama happens in the closing kilometers during the requisite bunch sprint of those competing for the Green jersey worn by the best sprinter, while the overall GC contenders stay safely back of the action. By contrast, the mountain stages, where the race is decided, offer dramatic race tactics, white-knuckled descents at 60+ mph, and lots and lots of suffering. To determine how "hard" a race is, you need to look at how much climbing the cyclists must do.

The simplest measure of the climbing done in any given year is to add the altitudes of all the peaks crossed during a race. But comparing the peaks of two mountains doesn't speak to the intensity of the effort required to climb over the top. For example, the highest peak climbed in the 2021 Tour de France was the Port d'Envalira in Andorra, at 2407 meters (7897 feet). However, the climb starts at an altitude of 1200 meters (3937 feet), providing a total vertical distance climbed of only 1207 meters (3960 feet). By contrast, the hardest climb of the 2021 race was Mont Ventoux in Provence at 1911 meters (6270 feet). With a base altitude of 308 meters (1010 feet), the total vertical distance ascended on Ventoux is 1603 meters (5259 feet). When we add to this that the Ventoux is only 21.4 kilometers long, compared to the more gradual 38.7 kilometers for the Port d'Envalira, although shorter, the Ventoux is clearly a more formidable, and steeper mountain to climb. The Tour de France began using a category system in 1947, that organized climbs into one of five groups with Category 4 being the easiest and Hors Category (HC) being the toughest. Hors Catégorie means beyond categorization in French. But this system is a subjective measure that has changed numerous times since its inception. For example, if a Category 1 climb happens at the end of a long stage, it is considered an HC climb for that day only.

Climb Score Ranking System

To generate an objective measure that allows for an apples-to-apples comparison between any two randomly selected climbs from any given year, I came up with my own ranking system that I call the Climb Score. The Climb Score is a unitless measure calculated as the product of the average grade of the climb and the horizontal distance covered in

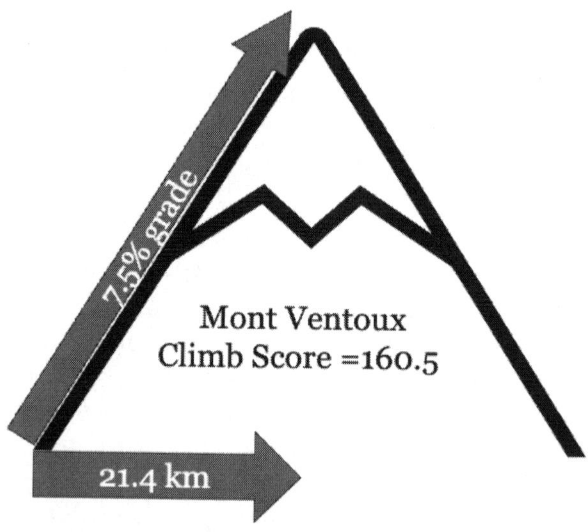

Figure 6. Mont Ventoux has one of the highest Climb Scores because it is both steep (7.5% avg. grade) and long, covering 21.4 km of horizontal distance from the base to the peak.

kilometers, from its base to its peak (Figure 6). For example, the average grade of Mont Ventoux is 7.5% and it covers 21.4 km, giving it a Climb Score of 160.5 (7.5 X 21.4 = 160.5). Like the category system used by ASO, I assigned climbs to one of five categories, (Table 3), with Category 5 being the easiest and Category 1 being the toughest. If you want to read my detailed explanation for how I scored and ranked each of the hills and mountains ever climbed in the Tour de France, all the information is in Appendix I in the back of the book.

Table 3. Climb categorization using the Climb Score.

Climb Category	Climb Score Range
Category 1	> 87.69
Category 2	72.89 – 87.68
Category 3	58.06 – 72.88
Category 4	43.23 – 58.05
Category 5	28.40 – 43.22

I plotted all the climb scores since 1950, after the interruption of World War II and at the beginning of the modern era of doping when athletes and team managers moved away from the simpler forms of doping with brandy, wine, and ether, and toward a more scientific approach centered on pharmaceuticals. Three spikes in the climb score are evident: 1951, 1973, and 1987 (Figure 7). What is really interesting is that each spike preceded the use of a new PED by most of the Peloton by a few years, e.g., amphetamines in 1952, cortisone in 1974, and EPO in 1990. Obviously, there is no way of knowing what percentage of the Peloton was using any drug at any given time, but based on hundreds of newspaper articles and books, one can make some rough estimations about the first time a drug was introduced and when it reached saturation in the Peloton.

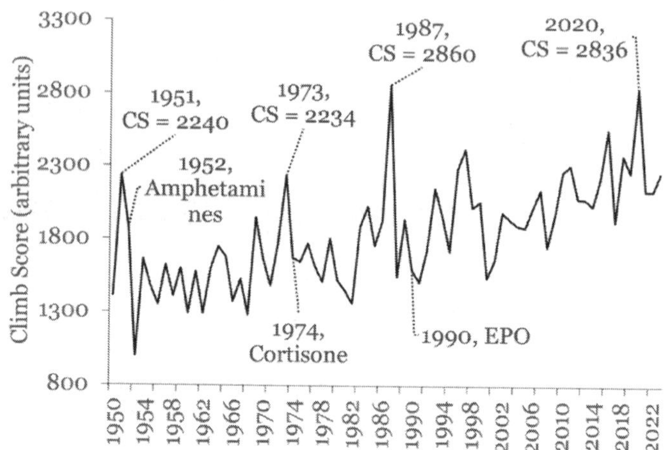

Figure 7. Following World War II, the average Climb Score (CS) of the Tour de France has progressively increased. There have been four spikes in CS, 1951, 1973, 1987, and 2020. The first three spikes preceded the introduction of a new PED to the Peloton.

Amphetamines

It is likely that amphetamines found their way into the Tour before 1952, there use having become normalized in everyday life after World War II when soldiers on both sides used them. But it wasn't until 1952 when Italian legend and WWII veteran Fausto Coppi admitted in an interview that he regularly used amphetamines during that year's Tour after finishing a disappointing 10th in the 1951 race, a route with a Climb Score of 2240, 22% higher than any race before it [2]. Coppi was an outspoken proponent of doping who, after his retirement said that most of the Peloton used amphetamines and *"those who say otherwise aren't worth talking to about cycling."* This also closely coincides with two other firsts for the Tour: the first television broadcast of the race took place during the final stage of the 1948 Tour [3], and the first ascent of the historic Alpe d'Huez, also in 1952.

Cortisone

Cortisone was first produced commercially around 1949 and found its way into to the Tour in the early to mid 1970s. By 1977 when another two-time winner, Bernard Thevenet, publicly admitted to using it during both wins in 1975 and 1977, cortisone was everywhere. *"I was doped by cortisone for three years and there were many like me."* As with amphetamines, the spread of cortisone throughout the Peloton followed a big jump in Climb Scores (2234) in 1973 [4].

Erythropoietin (EPO)

The modern era of doping in the Tour de France is divided into two periods, before and after the introduction of EPO into the Peloton. The ESPN, "30 for 30" documentary, *LANCE*, provides an excellent perspective of the evolution of doping from the use of what Lance Armstrong labelled *"Low octane"* doping techniques including amphetamines, cortisone, and testosterone, to the *"High octane, rocket fuel,"* that was EPO. Amphetamines and cortisone provided improvements in performance ranging between 0-5%, they are inconsistent between subjects and withdrawal symptoms during competition can severely impair endurance performance [5-7]. By contrast the response to EPO is rather consistent between subjects, improving performance by 8-12%, a staggering value that turned formerly unknown domestiques into Grand Tour contenders from one year to the next [8]. More importantly, the effects of EPO last for days to

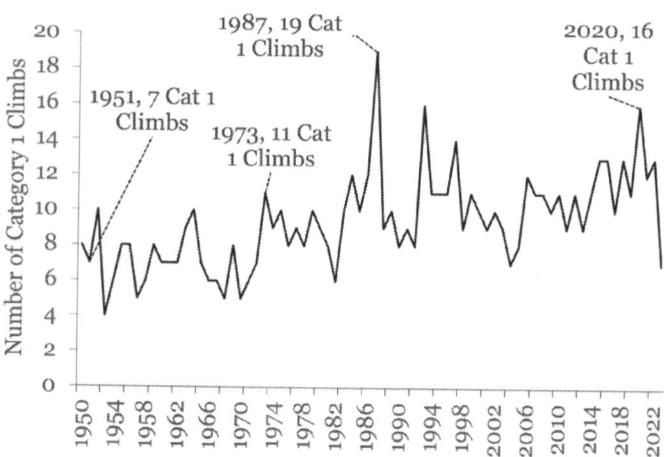

Figure 8. The number of Category 1 climbs in the Tour de France per year since 1950. The 1987 Tour not only had the most stages ever competed and the highest Climb Score, but it also had 19 Cat 1 level climbs, more than any other year. Unfortunately, 2020 was the second highest total with 16.

weeks and are much harder to detect in doping control tests than are amphetamines or cortisol. EPO stimulates the bone marrow to produce more red blood cells, boosting the delivery of oxygen to the muscles during high intensity aerobic exercise. This is particularly important when working in the high altitudes of the Pyrenees and Alps where the thinner air reduces the amount of oxygen that can be taken in with each breath. EPO was first used to treat anemia in 1987, and it was approved by the FDA for commercial use in 1989, a year before its first confirmed use in the Tour de France. In 2009, Dutch cyclist, Steven Rooks who finished second in the 1988 Tour while winning that year's King of the Mountains competition, admitted to using EPO starting at the end of the 1989 season [9]. He rode the Tour five more times between 1990-1994. Once again, like the introduction of amphetamines and cortisone, the arrival of EPO was preceded by a large spike in Climb Score. The 1987 race had a score of 2860. This is 28% higher than the value for the 1951 Tour, which was the second largest at the time, and an unbelievable 76% higher than the average Climb Score for all Tours de France between 1950 and 1986. But the Climb Score can be inflated by including lots of smaller, relatively easy climbs in succession. That's not what happened in 1987. The average number of Category 1 climbs in the Tours between 1950 and 1986 was approximately 8. The 1987 Tour de France had 19 Category 1 level climbs, more than any other race before or after (Figure 8).

Although there is not enough evidence to make the claim that these three significant increases in the Climb Score in 1951, 1973, and 1987 caused the Peloton to start using amphetamines, cortisone, and EPO respectively, it is reasonable to suggest that by making the race harder, organizers inadvertently played a role in driving the competitors to look for new ways to alleviate their suffering. So, were these spikes in difficulty by design or unfortunate coincidences? In each case, an argument can be made that the race organizers were trying to market a better, more dramatic event, and what says drama better than suffering over mountains?

The first live television broadcast from the Tour, and only the second of any French sporting event, happened during the final stage of the 1948 race at the Parc des Princes velodrome in Paris. Being well received, the race organizers wanted to capitalize on this success and expand the broadcast to include the mountain stages, which finally happened in 1958. To make their product more enticing to French national television, Tour organizers expanded the 1951 racecourse to include, for the first time, the Massif Central mountain range in south-central France, and the iconic Mont Ventoux in the Provence region of the Alps. This push for television exposure also coincided with a significant expansion of the Publicity Caravan that precedes the Peloton before it reaches each stage finish. Started in 1930 to reduce the influence of bicycle manufacturers while still supplying a steady stream of income from its corporate sponsors, the caravan grew exponentially during the post-war 1950s, into the 1960s [10].

By the 1970s, television coverage of the tour was a mix of live broadcasts from the locations of the first stage, the last stage, and a few mountain stages in between. The rest of the stages were broadcast on tape-delay. It was still in black and white. Tour organizers began a push to have the entire race broadcast live and in color. The first race to enjoy a completely live broadcast was 1972. The following year, the Tour was broadcast in bright, vibrant color for the first time, as it travelled over the second highest Climb Score to date.

The 1980s saw expansion of the Peloton to include entrants from non-European countries. Jonathan Boyer was the first American to enter the race in 1981. The same year, Australian Phil Anderson became the first non-European to wear the Yellow jersey. Then there was the American Greg LeMond, who placed third in his debut campaign in 1984, second in 1985, and became the first non-European to win the race in 1986. That same year the first American-based team, 7-Eleven, entered the race, with Alex Stieda wearing the Yellow jersey for one day, and Davis Phinney winning stage three. LeMond followed his victory in 1986 with two more wins in 1989 and 1990. Far from regarding it as an unfriendly invasion, the Tour organizers happily welcomed the new competitors, along with an influx of new television viewers, and the corporate advertising dollars (and francs) that came with them.

The 1987 Tour de France represents a confluence of several factors. After back-to-back drama-filled battles between French national hero and five-time winner Bernard Hinault and LeMond, his young American lieutenant, in 1985 (won by Hinault) and 1986 (won by LeMond), ASO hoped the 1987 race would be the cycling rubber match of the century. Unlike most Tour routes that are announced within a year of the start date, the 1987 course was unveiled on October 11, 1985. In honor of the 750th anniversary of its founding, the race would begin in West Berlin, on the other side of the Iron Curtain. In a show of Western capitalistic might, the Tour de France would spend the first five days in Germany, with three of them being in the Communist-controlled Eastern half of the country. Unfortunately, neither Hinault nor LeMond would race in 1987, Hinault having retired after the 1986 season, and LeMond recovering from a near-fatal hunting accident that left him with lead bird-shot pellets in his chest. In addition to having the highest Climb Score and the most Category 1 climbs of any Tour before or since, the 1987 race had 25 stages strung out over 26 days, also more than any Tour before or since. It was 4231 kilometers (2629 miles) in length, the longest race since 1970, and longer than any Tour since. ASO was determined to put on a great show, and they did, by making it the toughest Tour in the history of the race.

Despite not having their two top show ponies, the 1987 Tour de France was one of the best races in the long history of the event. Each of the top four finishers wore the Yellow jersey at least once. At the time it was the second closest finish in Tour history, a mere 40 seconds separating the winner, Irishmen Stephen Roche, from the Spaniard Pedro Delgado. The race was decided during a thrilling 21st stage from Le Bourg d'Oisans to La Plagne. The route took the Peloton over the three Category 1 climbs with the highest Climb Scores, the Col du Galibier (187.88), the Col de la Madeleine (152.47), and La Plagne (140.7). While wearing the Yellow jersey that he had stripped from Roche during the previous day's climb up Alpe d'Huez, Delgado attacked at the base La Plagne. Roche, fatigued from his own failed attack earlier in the day, chose to save his energy until the last two kilometers of the climb, when he threw everything he had into a counterattack. By the summit, Roche had reduced what was a three-minute deficit to less than five seconds. So exhausted by his efforts, Roche collapsed and was given oxygen before being airlifted to the nearest hospital. He was so disorientated after he woke up that he is quoted as saying, *"Everything is okay, mais pas de femme ce soir."* Translation... but no women this evening [11]. You can't make this stuff up.

Of the Tours de France that I have watched or read about, the 1987 version ranks second only to the 1989 race when Greg LeMond came back to beat his former teammate, and two-time winner, Frenchman Laurent Fignon by an even closer margin, eight seconds, on the final day's time trial. The Tour organizers had accomplished what they set out to do when planning the 1987 Tour. They grew American television viewership, providing a bridge until the return of LeMond in 1989. The last two wins by LeMond laid the foundation for what would be the Lance-Landis domination of the 2000s. But at what cost? Having lost the 1987 race, Delgado came back determined to do whatever was necessary to win the Tour in 1988. Shortly before the finish of the race that he dominated, winning by 7:13, he tested positive for the diuretic Probenecid, a masking agent used to flush out metabolites of steroid hormones before they can be detected in urine tests. Since Probenecid was not on the UCI's (cycling's governing body) banned list of substances, he kept his title [12]. In 1993, an Italian judicial investigation found that Roche had been administered EPO at the end of his career [13]. Was the 1987 so hard that it motivated riders to look for a doping advantage? What better than a new drug that was undetectable and could turn sprinters into climbers?

The most logical counterargument to my hypothesis is that PED will be used once they become available regardless of where you make the Peloton ride. But that narrative doesn't fit the chronology of the introduction of either amphetamines or cortisone into the Peloton, both of which had been available for decades before their use became widespread on the Tour. Even with EPO, this argument is shaky. Increasing the number of red blood cells as a method of athletic performance enhancement didn't begin with EPO. Instead, cyclists, and many other athletes, would have blood transfusions, either of the athlete's own blood (autologous) or that of a donor (homologous). Transfusions have been used in sports since the late 1960s at the latest. Dutchman Joop Zoetemelk, winner of 1980 Tour de France, admitted to receiving a homologous blood transfusion during the 1976 Tour, when he finished second [14]. The practice of receiving blood transfusions to boost performance was not banned by the IOC until 1985, largely in response to the outrage brought about by the US Men's Track Cycling Team's open use of the practice during the 1984 Summer Olympics in Los Angeles. Interestingly, once a reliable blood test for EPO was developed around 2000, most athletes who had been using it turned back to the old practice of autologous blood transfusion, by which they would reinfuse their own blood that had been removed from them a few weeks before the start of the race. EPO didn't make it possible to increase red blood cell levels, it just made it faster, easier, and much less dangerous.

A Warning for The Future?

During the drug-fueled free-for-all that marked the two decades from 1990 to 2010, when numerous athletes either tested positive or admitted to doping, the Climb Scores stayed relatively stable, averaging 1928. The one anomaly was the 1993 Tour (2420), when all three podium finishers were implicated in the use of EPO at some point during their careers. But then starting in 2011 the Climb Score started creeping up again, averaging 2254, with significant jumps in 2016 (2555) and 2020 (2836). Just like we saw after the 1987 spike when EPO changed the nature of the race, the last three years since the 2020 spike have included some fishy results that are hard to believe. Most of my suspicion revolves around the domination of the Peloton by the Dutch squad, Jumbo Visma.

In 2021, Tadej Pogačar won by a reasonable margin of 5:20 over Jonas Vingegaard. But he also won three of the four jerseys, taking the Yellow, White, and Polka Dot jerseys. The following year Vingegaard and Pogačar switched places and it was the performance of Vingegaard's teammate, Wout van Aert, that raised eyebrows when he won the Green jersey by a huge margin and placed fifth in the King of the Mountains competition. To be able to compete so highly with both the climbers AND sprinters is unusual to say the least. Van Aert also wore the Yellow jersey for four days early in the race and had three individual stage wins, all while sacrificing himself for his team leader. I find his performance too good to be clean. The icing on the cake was the disqualification of the sixth-place finisher, Columbian Nairo Quintana, after he tested positive for Tramadol, an opioid pain killer that was very popular in the Peloton before it was banned by the UCI in 2019. This was the first time that a top-ten finisher had been disqualified for a doping offense since 2012.

Then came the 2023 Grand Tour season. Depending on your vantage point, the results from the summer of 2023 were either magical or dubious. First on the calendar was the Giro d'Italia in May, won in dramatic fashion on the second to last day by Slovenian and Jumbo Visma rider Primož Roglič. The penultimate stage was a mountain time trial. Trailing Welshman Geraint Thomas by 26 seconds, Roglič won the stage by 40 seconds despite having to dismount half-way up the mountain to put his chain back on after hitting a pothole. The 14-second margin of victory was the second smallest in the history of the race.

Next came the Tour de France where Vingegaard and Pogačar duked it out again, going toe to toe for the first two weeks of the race. Prior to the last mountain time trial, a short 13.9-mile sprint in the Alps, Vingegaard led Pogačar by just 10 seconds. As is custom, Pogačar went second to last while Vangegaard, in the Yellow jersey followed two minutes later. Before either man set off the leader on the day was van Aert who had ridden a powerful second half of the time trial. Pogačar beat van Aert's time by 1:13, a sizable margin, but one that made sense because of all the extra work that van Aert had already done during this first two weeks of the Tour while defending Vingegaard's lead.

But then Vingegaard upped the ante and absolutely demolished everyone, beating Pogačar by a whopping 1:38. My first thought was that this was reminiscent of when Lance Armstrong took more than a minute out of Jan Ulrich during the 2005 prolog. The margin of victory was too much, especially when you saw the contrast of the two riders on the screen after they each finished the stage: Pogačar looked like he was about to die while Vingegaard looked relatively fresh. As shocking as that stage was, the next day's mountain stage was even worse. What was supposed to be the final showdown between the Pogačar and Vingegaard turned into a slaughter when Pogačar cracked on the final climb and Vingegaard turned the last screws to seal his second Tour win in as many years. Part of the deficit was because Pogačar fell early in the stage, but he shouldn't have lost to Vingegaard by 5:47 on the day.

The last of the three Grand Tours is the Vuelta a España. American Sepp Kuss, also of Jumbo Visma won. In second and third place were Jonas Vingegaard and Primož Roglič. That's right, all three podium positions were occupied by members of the same team. This has only happened one other time since 1962 when the Tour went back to hosting sponsored teams instead of national teams. In 1966 the top three finishers of the Vuelta were members of the Spanish team, Kas. But unlike the 2023 Vuelta which started with 22 teams and 176 riders, the 1966 race only had nine teams and 90 riders, greatly increasing the possibility of a podium sweep.

So, Jumbo Visma not only won all three of the Grand Tours, something that has never happened before, but all three of the winners finished on the podium in Madrid. This is the textbook definition of a dominant team. What's most unbelievable is the fact that Kuss had enough left in the tank to win the Vuelta after sacrificing himself for Roglič in the Giro and Vingegaard in the Tour. Although I suspect that his two teammates pulled their punches a bit in the Vuelta to pay Kuss back for all he did to help them win their races, it's still an incredible feat to ride three Grand Tours well and still have enough reserve to win a Grand Tour.

The domination exhibited by Jumbo Visma is reminiscent of how Lance Armstrong's U.S. Postal and Discovery Channel teams ruled the Tour de France Peloton for seven years. No one riding for U.S. Postal or Discovery Channel (the team's title sponsor after U.S. Postal Service stopped in 2005) ever tested positive for PED while a member of those teams. But by 2012 no fewer than 12 former members had admitted to using EPO between 1998-2006 [15]. Unfortunately, the same can't be said for Jumbo Visma during the summer of 2023. One of their up-and-coming youngsters, German Michel Hessmann tested positive for a banned diuretic during an out-of-competition test on June 14th [16]. Hessmann rode in support of Roglič during the Giro, finishing a strong 33rd overall. The matter is under investigation be the UCI and German authorities. Of course, the actions of one member don't necessarily mean that his teammates are engaging in similar behavior. But I for one have seen this movie before and I know how it usually ends. Most often, where there is smoke, and there was a LOT of smoke floating around Jumbo Visma in 2023, there is usually a fire, maybe two or three.

In the interest of being cautious with my inferences I will again admit that what I have shown here is not ironclad evidence of a relationship between the difficulty of the athletic event and increased incidence of doping. But a pattern clearly exists. When the Climb Score increases suspicious results are not far behind. Race organizers should consider the potential consequences of making the most beautiful bicycle races in the world into human cock fights of attrition and suffering. Everyone wants to see the best cyclists in the world duke it out over the Aubisque and the Tourmalet (a name that translates to *"Evil Trip"*), but we should take heed from the lessons of history that show us what can happen when we push athletes too far. As is the case with many things in life, more is not always better.

Reference:

1. Reeth, D.V., *Road Cycling TV Viewing Report 2019*. 2019, Katholieke Universiteit Leuven.
2. Fotheringham, W., *Fallen Angel: The Passion of Fausto Coppi*. 2010, London, England, UK: Yellow Jersey Press.
3. *The Tour de France 1903-2003: A Century of Sporting Structures, Meanings and Values*. 2003, London, England, UK: Frank Cass.
4. Mondenard, J.-P.d., *Dopage: L'imposture des Performances*. 2000, Paris, France: Éditions Chiron.
5. A. Arlettaz, K.C., H. Portier, A.M. Lecoq, A. Pelle, J. de Ceaurriz, *Effects of Acute Prednisolone Intake During Intense Submaximal Exercise*. International Journal of Sports Medicine, 2006. **27**(9): p. 673-679.
6. Dmitry V Zaretsky, M.B.B., Maria V Zaretskaia, Pamela J Durant, and Daniel E Rusyniak, *The Ergogenic Effect of Amphetamine*. Temperature. **1**(3): p. 242-247.
7. Wyndham, C.H., et al., *Physiological Effects of the Amphetamines During Exercise*. South African Medical Journal, 1974. **45**(2): p. 247-252.
8. Philippe Connes, S.P., Alain Varray, Christian Préfaut, Corinne Caillaud, *Faster Oxygen Uptake Kinetics at the Onset of Submaximal Cycling Exercise Following 4 Weeks Recombinant Human Erythropoietin (r-HuEPO) Treatment*. European Journal of Physiology, 2003. **447**: p. 231-238.

9. Smeets, M., *Het Laatste Geel (The Last Yellow)*. 2009, Amsterdam, Netherlands: Nieuw Amsterdam Uitgevers.
10. Luke Edwards-Evans, S.L., Andy McGrath, *The Official History of the Tour de France*. 2021, London, England, UK: Wellbeck.
11. Ryan, B., *The Ascent*. 2018, Dublin, Ireland: Gill Books.
12. Startt, J., *The Great Pedro Delgado*, in *VeloNews*. 2023, Outside: Boulder, Coloroado, USA.
13. McRae, D., *Stephen Roche: I Had People Spitting Rice and Wine in my Face*, in *The Guardian*. 2012, Guardian Media Group: London, England, UK.
14. McKay, F., *A History on Blood Transfusions in Cycling, Part 2*, in *CyclingNews*. 2013, Future: Bath, England, UK.
15. (USADA), U.S.A.-D.A., *Reasoned Decision of the United States Anti-Doping Agency on Disqualification and Ineligibility*. 2012.
16. O'Shea, S., *Michel Hessmann Under Criminal Investigation by German Authorities After Diuretic Positive*, in *VeloNews*. 2023, Outside: Boulder, Colorado, USA.

Chapter 5. How the Steroid Era Saved Baseball

"Chicks dig the long ball."– ***Tom Glavine, Atlanta Braves Pitcher***

Of the four major sports leagues in the United States, only one, Major League Baseball (MLB), doesn't have a hard salary cap. The salary cap places a ceiling on the amount a money that each team can spend on players' salaries each year. When combined with revenue sharing between teams, a salary cap makes it more likely that teams in smaller TV markets like Kansas City, Oakland, and Tampa Bay can compete with those from the larger markets, e.g., New York, Los Angeles, and Chicago. The argument for a salary cap is that it creates parity, making for a healthier, more robust league. The more cynical view is that a salary cap puts artificial restraints on the free market and takes money out of the pockets of the players and puts it into the hedge funds of the owners. It was this fundamental disagreement between players and owners that led to the longest work stoppage in baseball history, and set the stage for the Steroid Era, during which owners turned a blind eye to the rampant use of performance enhancing drugs, only to later castigate these same players when it served their purposes of *"cleaning up the game of baseball."*

On August 12, 1994, MLB players walked off the job. It was the fifth work stoppage for baseball in 22 years and it would be the longest, lasting 232 days. The strike led to the cancellation of the 1994 World Series, only the second time (1904) that the series was not played at the end of the season. The most obvious consequence of the strike was the immediate financial loss suffered by both sides, the owners lost ticket sales and TV revenue, while the players went without pay for 30% of the season. But the most lasting repercussion of the strike was the alienation of the fans, hardworking, middle-class Americans who had no interest in making allies with either side of a fight between millionaires and billionaires.

Between 1985 and 1994, baseball experienced a period of rapid growth in average attendance, increasing by over 40%, and reaching its peak in 1994 (31,256 per game) [1]. The strike brought a sudden reversal of fortunes. Average attendance in 1995 plummeted by almost 20% from the prior year, and it didn't recover completely until 2006 (Appendix II). What baseball needed was the ultimate feel-good story to help their fans forget the strike and remember why they loved the great American pastime. That's exactly what they got in 1998 when Mark McGwire and Sammy Sosa took the league and all its fans on a ride that would rewrite the record books.

Although all sports celebrate their records, few do so like baseball. More than any other game, baseball is driven by statistics. One hundred and sixty-two games each season provide a huge sample size to compile meaningful data. Because of this, baseball allows for comparisons between players of different eras. Some notable records include the longest hitting streak (Joe DiMaggio, 56 games), most career hits (Pete Rose, 4256), and most consecutive games played over a career (Cal Ripken Jr., 2632). But the mark that is arguably the most important to most baseball fans is the single season home run record.

The home run is a play like no other in sports. Unlike a buzzer beater in basketball or a Hail Mary in football, once the bat contacts the ball, the outcome of the play is understood by everyone in the stadium. The opposing players can only crane their necks and watch as the ball soars overhead, into the outstretched arms of the fans in the outfield seats. Depending on which team you're supporting, the power and finality of a home run inspires fits of ecstasy and crushing, shocked silence. I've experienced these home-run-induced emotional extremes on several occasions, particularly during the 2019 MLB post-season. During game six of the American League Championship Series (ALCS), my Houston Astros were tied with the New York Yankees 4-4 in the bottom of the ninth inning when Jose Altuve slapped a high fastball from the Yankees closer Aroldis Chapman off the left field wall in Minute Maid Park. That walk-off, two run homer sent the Astros to their third World Series in team history.

Before the pitch you could hear a low din of muttering voices in the capacity crowd. Even from the limited vantage point provided by the TV camera, as soon as I heard the crack of the bat, I knew that ball was gone, and so did everyone else watching. The stadium erupted in a roar loud enough to shake the cameras. The images of Altuve trotting around the infield were literally shaking all around the screen because of the cacophony of sound produced by the crazed home crowd.

But just 11 days later the script was flipped as I watched Howie Kendrick of the Washington Nationals crank a ball into the right corner during game seven of the World Series. This time the muttering of the crowd at Minute Made Park was abruptly interrupted by stunned silence as everyone held their collective breath and willed the ball to fade foul. Instead, it slammed into the right field foul pole with a loud, unmistakable *"CLUNG!"* Despite the fact that the Astros have made two more trips to the World Series, winning it in 2022, the sting of Kendrick's homer hasn't faded from my memory.

Babe Ruth hit 60 home runs during the 1927 season. It took 34 years before Roger Maris hit 61 during the 1961 season. Baseball would have to wait another 37 years before the record would be broken again. In April of 1998, I was teaching high school biology and algebra, and coaching water polo and swimming. The Oilers had abandoned Houston for Nashville, Tennessee the year prior. The Rockets were three years removed from winning their second consecutive NBA championship and were rapidly aging. But the Astros were coming off their first trip to the post-season since 1986 and were favored to win the National League Central division. The Astros would finish with a record of 102-60, at the time a team record for most wins in a season. Although baseball was my third favorite of the major sports to watch, above all else I am a fan of athletics, and a homer, I love all things Houston, even Rice University (Go Coogs!).

But the anticipation for the new baseball season extended well beyond Houston. Across the country, for the first time in several seasons, baseball fans were cautiously optimistic for opening day. Their focus was centered on St. Louis, Missouri where the year before, Cardinals' slugger Mark McGwire had hit 58 home runs, the closest anyone had come to Roger Maris' record of 61. In most instances record chases are solo affairs. One athlete, alone, challenging for his immortal legacy. But 1998 would be different. There was a second challenger to the home run record, Chicago Cubs outfielder, Sammy Sosa. The presence of this specific second challenger exponentially amplified the impact that the 1998 record chase had on the mood of the fans, capturing the imagination of even the most jaded, and erasing all memory of the 1994 strike.

There were several factors that made Mark McGwire and Sammy Sosa the perfect cast members for this story, the first being the teams for which they played. St. Louis and Chicago are quintessential mid-western American cities. They have long-standing, loyal fan bases, extending back to the earliest days of baseball. The Cardinals were established in 1882, and joined the National League ten years later, while the Cubs were charter members of the league when it started in 1876. These were not expansion teams. But nor were they teams from either coast whose fans have been known to arrive at games late and leave early. Much of the rivalry is caused by the difference in size between the two cities. In 1998 St. Louis had around 340,000 residents while Chicago's population was 2.8 million. But what St. Louis lacked in size it made for in championships. By 1998, St. Louis had won nine World Series while Chicago had won only two with the last coming 90 years earlier. Best of all, the Cubs and Cardinals are hated rivals who compete in the same division, facing each other 11 times during the 1998 season. At the time, they were also in the same division as my Astros, giving me six opportunities each to watch McGwire and Sosa try and blast moon shots into the upper deck of the Astrodome. McGwire would hit number 32 in Houston, Sosa would get numbers 47 and 66, the latter a game I was lucky enough to attend.

Beyond the teams and the cities they represented were the two players, who could not have been more different, yet complimentary. Mark McGwire was a red headed, southern Californian who started his baseball career as a pitcher before becoming a hitter while playing at the University of Southern California. He won a silver medal representing the United States at the Los Angeles Olympics in 1984 [2]. By contrast, Sammy Sosa was born in a company town owned by one of the many sugar mills in the Dominican Republic. After his father died when Sosa was seven years old, his family was forced to live in an abandoned hospital. He began playing organized baseball at the age of 14, using a mitt made from a milk carton, a rolled-up sock fashioned into a baseball, and tree branch in lieu of a bat [3]. While McGwire came from relative privilege (his father was a dentist), Sosa sold oranges and shined shoes to help his mother support his six siblings.

Upon arrival in the MLB, McGwire saw immediate success, setting a rookie record for home runs in a season (49) with the Oakland A's in 1987. He followed that up with a World Series title in 1989. Sosa had a slower start to his career, playing three unremarkable seasons for the Texas Rangers (1989) and Chicago White Sox (1990-1991) before making his way to the Cubs prior to the 1992 season. Whereas most baseball fans expected McGwire to make a run at Maris's record in 1998 after hitting 58 the previous season, Sosa came out of nowhere, his previous best being 40 homers in 1996. Finally, there was the differences in their personalities. Although McGwire was neither shy nor unfriendly, he was a man of relatively few words. By mid-season, he had grown noticeably frustrated with reporters, not because he didn't want to speak with them or answer their questions, but because he was tired of talking about the same thing, the home run record. On the other end of the spectrum was Sosa who loved interacting with both the media and fans.

The baseball season is six months long, running from April through September. To have a fighting chance of topping 60 home runs you have to average ten homers a month. McGwire was ready for the start of the season, hitting 27 home runs by the end of May. Sosa had only 13, which was still on pace for 38 home runs for the season, close to his career best from two years before. But then Sosa set a record for the most home runs in a month, smashing 20 dingers in June, a record that still stands. By the end of June, McGwire was at 37 while Sosa was right behind him at 33. For the rest of the season the gap was never more than seven. There were seven ties and four lead changes.

When September rolled around both men were approaching the record of 61. McGwire hit his 60th, tying the immortal Babe Ruth on September 5th. Sosa kept pace, hitting his 58th on the same day. Then the baseball gods smiled on the entire game, and everyone associated with it. Next on the schedule was a two-game series between the Cubs and Cardinals in St. Louis. You couldn't make this stuff up if you tried. The buildup to these games was like what you see for the Super Bowl. The press pit included journalists from all over the globe, including countries that rarely follow baseball. The press-conference before the first game included both players sitting shoulder to shoulder, sharing one mic, cracking jokes, and totally enjoying each other's company. At one point a reporter commented that considering how they had both come from such different backgrounds as children, could they ever have envisioned themselves being present in such settings? Sosa immediately leaned into the microphone and said, *"Not really, but I have to say, baseball been berry berry good to me."* Everyone let out a big laugh while McGuire followed up with, *"God bless American, right?"* Sosa finished the levity with, *"What a country."* It was clear while watching this exchange that this was not an act. Despite their competitive natures, these two men were able to compartmentalize their egos long enough to make the moment special. It was evident that these two men genuinely liked each other.

Although Major League Baseball could not have planned the two-game series between these two old rivals as the setting for the culmination of a two-man race to rewrite the record books, they didn't waste the opportunity to make it an absolute spectacle. The games were broadcast across the country and around the world. According to Fox Sports, 43.1 million Americans tuned in to watch the second game, on a Tuesday night [4]. If either of the two men broke the record, the MLB had planned for a ceremony after the game to mark the event. But the best part of the two days was the presence of Roger Maris' family in the stands, guests of the St. Louis Cardinals and MLB.

1961 was an expansion year in baseball. The league added two new teams, the Washington Senators (later becoming the Minnesota Twins) and Los Angeles Angels. It would add two more the next year, the Houston Colt .45s (later becoming my Astros) and the New York Mets. The addition of four teams required a longer regular season (162 games) to balance the schedule. When Babe Ruth set the record of 60 home runs in 1927, the baseball season was 154 games long. This put the MLB in a sticky situation when it became clear that Maris would challenge the record in 1961. In stark contrast to how the MLB promoted the 1998 record chase as a renewal of baseball, in 1961, then Commissioner, Ford C. Frick decreed that for Maris' record to be considered official he would have to set it in 154 games. Unfortunately, it took Maris 158 games to tie Ruth's record, and the full 162 to break it. In response, Commissioner Frick put an asterisk next to Maris' mark and refused to recognize it as the official record. Fortunately, this error in judgment was corrected in

1991. Sadly, Maris didn't live to see this day, having died in 1985.

As you might expect, the controversy surrounding his 1961 record chase made it a stressful affair for Maris. Half of his own New York fan base didn't want him to break the record of the former Yankee great, viewing it as almost sacrilegious. It has been reported that the stress of the record chase caused Maris lose weight and a modest amount of hair [5]. The MLB would correct its mistake in 1998. Not only were Sammy Sosa and Mark McGwire supported and celebrated throughout their respective campaigns, but the MLB embraced Maris' family, celebrating his record posthumously as it should have been in his lifetime.

On September 7th, the first game started at 1:11 PM. Hitting third in the bottom of the first inning, McGwire came to the plate. The first pitch was a slider away that McGwire missed badly. The second pitch was a high fastball that missed the strike zone. The third pitch was left out over the plate, right in McGwire's sweet spot. He belted it 430 feet into left field between the second and third decks, just to the left of the McDonald's sign for Big Mac Land, a pun on McGwire's name. As he rounded the bases, the camera caught Sosa give a gentle fist pump and a golf clap. Both the Cubs 1st baseman Mark Grace and 3rd baseman Gary Gaetti delivered celebratory high fives as McGwire stepped on their respective bags. McGwire's 10-year-old son, Matthew, a Cardinal's bat boy, was waiting for his dad at home plate where he was scooped off his feet right into an enormous bear hug. McGwire then pointed into the stands where his father, John McGwire was sitting, watching his son hit his 61st home run of the season, tying the record that had stood since 1961, on what was his father's 61st birthday. If you made a movie with this plot line, no one would believe it. The Cardinals went on to win the game 3-2. The second game would be played during prime time the following evening.

On Tuesday, September 8th I was coaching my boy's water polo team from Strake Jesuit College Prep to a win over Baytown Sterling high school. Our parents in the stands were providing a steady feed of the events as they played out on a hand-held Sony Watchman. When I got home that night I watched the game, having taught myself how to program a TV recording on my VCR. Today's technology is so much easier than what we had to deal with in the late 90s.

In the bottom of the fourth inning with the Cubs leading 2-0, McGwire came up to bat. The first pitch from Steve Trachsel was low and slightly outside, a pitch McGwire would normally lay off for a ball. But he was able to reach down with what looked more like a golf swing to catch enough of the ball to send it screaming down the left field line. It cleared the wall by just a few inches. The noise that erupted was a combination of screams and fireworks. Thinking he may have only hit a double McGwire began his trip around the bases at a sprint. In his excitement he missed tagging first base and was called back by his first base coach. This time the entire Cubs' infield congratulated him as he jogged around the diamond.

Before McGwire reached home plate, the Cubs' catcher, Steve Servais gave him a hardy handshake followed by a man-hug. After lifting Matthew high into the air, McGwire was mobbed by his entire team. More high fives and hugs followed. Then Sosa, having made his way from his defensive position in right field found McGwire to congratulate him. McGwire wrapped his arms around Sosa's waist and lifted him into the air as Sosa embraced him and slapped him on the back several times. Finally, the two men performed each other's signature celebrations. First, they did McGwire's two-fisted, double high five, followed by a right upper cut to the chest. Then they did Sosa's move, blowing two kisses with two fingers and tapping their hearts twice. Next, McGwire spotted the Maris family just to the right of the Cardinal's dugout sitting with a group of baseball dignitaries and VIPs. McGwire hopped over the wall and embraced each of Maris' five children. Finally, McGwire took the microphone and addressed everyone in attendance.

> *"All my family, everybody, my son, Chicago Cubs, Sammy Sosa, Unbelievable. Class. Thank you, St. Louis!"*

If all this wasn't enough, what happened to the most famous ball in all of sporting history was the final fortuitous twist to make this story truly unbelievable. As McGwire and Sosa got closer to the record, the scrums for the home run balls got progressively more violent and dangerous. Because of this, extra security was on hand for both games. The planned procedure was to rush security to where the ball had been hit, surround the lucky fan who ended up with the ball, and hustle them into a waiting area where they could wait for the post-game ceremony in safety. Since his record breaking 62nd homer was a line drive that barely cleared the left field wall, no fans ever had a chance to get close to it. Instead, it bounced around in an area occupied by members of the grounds crew who had gathered by a gate in left field, ready to clear confetti and other debris from the field during the celebration that followed the record setting blast. Rather than a crush of fans collapsing on one poor soul, the ball was grabbed by Tim Forneris, a 22-year-old computer programmer who was moonlighting at Busch stadium for $40 a day [6]. After it cleared the wall, Forneris only had to beat his older brother to the ball. Then he stuffed it in his pocket right before he and the rest of the crew raced onto the field for cleanup duty. As he was running around bailing the streamers falling from the upper decks, he had a ball worth at least a million dollars in his pocket. After months of speculation as to how much the Cardinals, the MLB, or McGwire himself would have to shell out to get the treasured ball from a fan, Forneris asked for nothing. With complete grace and humility, he addressed McGwire and everyone in attendance when he was brought onto the temporary stage that was the focus of the post-game ceremony.

> *"Mr. McGwire, I think I have something that belongs to you."*

The game ended in a 6-3 win for the Cardinals. Mark McGwire was the new single-season king of home runs. But that was only the race to break Maris' record. Unlike in 1961 when Maris set the record on the last day of the season, it only took McGwire 145 games to hit his 62nd home run. There were still 17 games left in the 1998 baseball season and Sammy Sosa was only four home runs behind. The race to set the new record was still going strong. Between September 11th and 13th, Sosa hit a home run in four consecutive games against the Milwaukee Brewers. At the same time McGwire suffered through a mini slump, hitting no dingers over his next five games including a three-game series in Houston, (luckily, I was not in attendance). They were now tied at 62 homer runs.

On Friday, September 25th, tied with McGwire at 65 home runs, Sosa and the Cubs arrived in Houston for a three-game series. I had unbreakable weekend plans with my girlfriend at the time, so this my only chance to see one of these giants contribute to the annals of baseball history. From my seat in the lower deck in right field I was well-positioned for a chance to catch any ball that came my way. In the top of the 4th inning with the Astros up 2-1, Sosa came to the plate. He turned on an inside fast ball from our ace, Jose Lima, and blasted it into the small middle deck in the left field. He was now in the lead with his 66th home run of the season.

After the excitement abated and the Astros came up to bat again in the bottom of the fourth, I began noticing that every second or third person was either listening to the radio or watching a handheld TV. I knew that serious baseball fans did this all the time as the radio commentary is a nice compliment to watching a game in a loud stadium at a distance from the action. But I also knew that most, if not all, of these fans were listening to the Cardinals playing the Montreal Expos in St. Louis. A few minutes later I started hearing the mutterings that McGwire had hit his 66th to draw even again.

Sosa had no more luck against my Astros. His chase of the record would stop at 66 home runs. A number that most thought unattainable was now only good enough to be tied with another man in the same season. But McGwire was not finished. He ended the season with an offensive explosion, hitting his 67th and 68th on Saturday, and his 69th and 70th on Sunday, September 27th, 1998. The last day of the regular season.

When Babe Ruth hit his 60th home run in 1927, he broke his own record by one run. Thirty-four years later Roger Maris nudged the record up to 61. In 1998 Sammy Sosa pushed the needle ahead by five runs, and that was only good enough for second place! Mark McGwire had obliterated the previous mark. The old record hadn't been broken by a lean at the tape, it had been eclipsed by NINE runs! Going from 61 to 70 is an increase of almost 15%, a statistic that is almost unheard of in clean sports. Foreshadowing...

Baseball was saved by the events of the 1998 season. Average attendance increased by 16% compared to 1995, the year immediately following the strike of 1994. But all those good feelings and the euphoric high they produced would come crashing back to Earth a few short years later, as the American public in general, and the management of Major League Baseball in particular, would turn their collective backs on the heroes of that summer in a show of self-righteous indignation.

In 2001, San Francisco Giants' slugger Barry Bonds, jealous of the attention that McGwire and Sosa had received three years earlier, began his own assault on the home run record [7]. He would set a new mark of 73 that still stands.

But unlike McGwire and Sosa, Bonds had a contentious relationship with the media and fans that prevented his 2001 campaign from capturing the imagination of the American public. To the contrary, it made many people vocally suspicious of the source of his new slugging prowess, having hit no more than 49 homers in any other season. In four short years between 1998 and 2001, the once untouchable benchmark of 61 home runs had been surpassed six times, three times by Sosa (66 in 1998, 63 in 1999, and 64 in 2001), twice by McGwire (70 in 1998 and 65 in 1999), and finally by Bonds. A two-year investigation of Bonds revealed that he had been using two anabolic steroids since at least 2001 and that he had obtained them from his personal trainer, who in turn had gotten them from the Bay Area Laboratory Co-Cooperative (BALCO). On September 3rd, 2003, federal agents raided the offices of BALCO, confiscating records that fingered athletes from several sports including track and field, football, and, of course, baseball. Congressional hearings on the use of steroids in baseball would follow in 2005.

The whole sordid tale would reach its miserable conclusion on March 17th, 2005 when in separate hearings, players, their labor union (Donald Fehr, MLB Player's Association Executive Director 1983-2009), and management (Bud Selig, Commissioner 1992-2015), took turns being grilled by a bipartisan House oversight committee of angry congressmen and women who were, above all else, worried about the impact of steroid use on the impressionable youth of the country. The players went first. From left to right on the CSPAN broadcast were Jose Canseco, Sammy Sosa, Mark McGwire, Rafael Palmeiro, and pitcher Curt Schilling who didn't add much to the events of the day.

- Canseco was a former teammate of McGwire's when they played for the Oakland A's in the late 1980s and early 1990s. He had released a tell-all *mea culpa* memoir in 2005 titled *"Juiced"* in which he admitted to his own steroid use and named several other players who he said he had direct knowledge of their steroid use. One of the more incendiary passages was a claim that he and McGwire would inject each other with steroids in the clubhouse bathroom stalls before games, a claim that McGwire has always denied [8].

- Next came Sammy Sosa. Despite the fact that by 2005 there were easily thousands of hours of video evidence that he could speak English quite fluently, he showed up with a translator. Oh, and of course, a lawyer too. Beside the ludicrous spectacle he made of himself with his legal and linguistic chaperones, his testimony was unremarkable.
- The saddest testimony came from McGwire who, when asked pointed questions about his use of a steroid precursor called Androstenedione, which was perfectly legal in 1998, refused to answer, instead meekly stating repeatedly that he, "*was not here to talk about the past, but to be positive about the future.*" Whatever the hell that means.
- But the testimony that summed up the Steroid Era of baseball was provided by Rafael Palmeiro, who had also been named by Canseco in <u>*Juiced*</u> as a steroid user. During his opening statement to the committee, Palmeiro wagged his finger at the congresswomen and men and stated firmly, "*Let me start by telling you this: I have never used steroids, period. I do not know how to say it any more clearly than that. Never. The reference to me in Mr. Canseco's book is absolutely false.*" Less than six months later, Palmeiro was suspended after failing a drug test for the steroid Stanozolol. The test was administered on May 4th. Palmeiro claimed that he had received a vial of Vitamin B12 from his teammate Miguel Tejada [9]. Tejada later testified that he had brought the vials of B12 back with him from the Dominican Republic, which makes no sense since in 2005 this was a substance that any

training staff had on hand and would gladly provide injections of without question. Instead, Palmeiro insists to this day that he took the vial of Dominican B12, a syringe, and a needle provided by Tejada home and had his wife inject him. The ink of the new MLB drug testing and suspension policy was barely dry when Palmeiro became only the sixth player suspended for using PED.

The tale of Rafael Palmeiro indicates just how bad the steroid problem in baseball must have been at its height. When you consider that Palmeiro received his vial of Dominican B12 from Tejada sometime in mid-April, just a few weeks after proclaiming his steadfast innocence, under oath, in response to a Congressional subpoena, you can extrapolate that remarkably brazen behavior to an entire league of entitled, unregulated men who are grossly overpaid for playing a child's game.

But as much as I cringed while watching Mark McGwire blather on about being adopting a positive attitude for the future, I completely understood his unwillingness to incriminate himself. None of those men were offered immunity for their testimony. At the time, the statute of limitation for the illegal use of steroids was five years, and it was punishable by up to a year in federal prison. Not I, nor anyone I know would do anything other than plead the fifth under those circumstances. So as embarrassing as his performance was, at least McGwire didn't perjure himself. There is reasonable evidence that both Sosa and Palmeiro did.

As cringeworthy as the players' testimony was, it paled in comparison to how infuriating it was to listen to Commissioner Bud Selig. Selig became acting Commissioner in 1992, one year after his predecessor, Fay Vincent penned an official memo that made steroid use against the spirit of the game of baseball. But even though he was at the helm during the meat of the Steroid Era, he insisted during an exchange with then representative Bernie Sanders, that he didn't know that there was any steroid problem in baseball until 1998.

> **Sanders**: *I gather that if you have made tremendous progress [with eliminating steroids from baseball] there must have been a tremendous problem.*
>
> **Selig**: *Did we have a major problem? No, I don't believe we ever had what he says [Jose Canseco in his book, Juiced] is a major problem. There is no concrete evidence of that. There is no testing evidence. There is no other kind of evidence. Nobody ever came to me. No manager, no general manager ever came to me in the 90's. I became concerned myself in July on a Sunday morning when I read about Mark McGwire and Andro.*

Holy guacamole... Where to begin.

- Let's start with the claim that there was no testing evidence of a steroid problem in baseball in the 1990s. No kidding!? Baseball DID NOT test for steroids until the 2003 season, so of course there was no testing evidence!
- Next there is the claim that there was no concrete evidence of a steroid problem. I strenuously disagree. As commissioner it was Bud Selig's job to monitor the game for any anomalies that would appear to be changing the game, for better or worse, and during the Steroid Era the home run was transforming the game. There are two ways to look at data related to performance metrics like home runs, total home runs hit across the league, and the performance of the stat leaders. During Bud Selig's first year as commissioner

in 1992 there were 3038 home runs across the league. Over the next six seasons ending in 1998, when he said he first thought there might be a problem, there were never fewer than 4030 (1993), with a peak of 5064 homers in 1998 (Appendix II). That is an increase of 66.7% in just six seasons! As for the assessment of the individual performers, the most commonly used benchmark is the number of players hitting 40 or more home runs in a season (Figure 9). In 1992 there were only two players who hit 40 or more home runs. By 1996, there were a whopping 17 players who reached this milestone. That's an increase of 750%. This metric stayed elevated until 2007, four years after the league began testing for steroids.

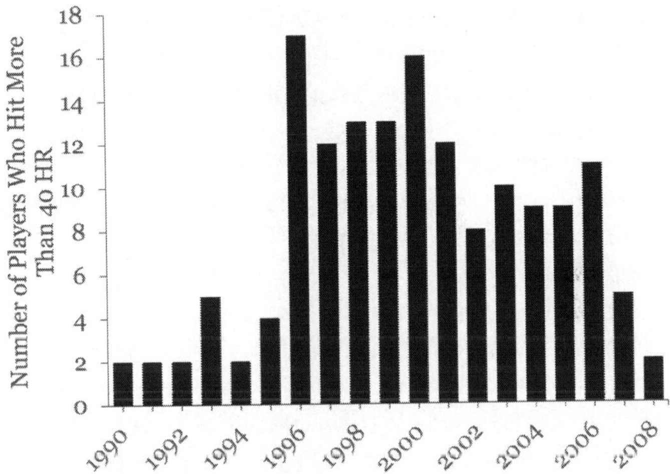

Figure 9. The number of players who hit at least 40 home runs exploded in the heart of the Steroid Era of baseball in 1996 and remained unusually high until three years after PED testing started in 2004.

- If this isn't evidence enough, we can look at the number of players who have hit 50 or more home runs in a season. I picked this number because for a player to be considered a threat to break the record of 61 home runs in a season, they have to hit at least 50. Between 1920, when Babe Ruth hit 54 home runs and 1961 when Roger Maris hit 61, the 50 HR milestone was reached 15 times, that's once every 2.7 seasons. Between 1961 and 1998, when Mark McGwire hit 70, the 50 HR mark was reached 13 times, a similar pace of once every 2.8 seasons. But when we look at the pace set during the Steroid Era, the numbers become comical. Between 1992-1998, before Selig says he suspected there might be a problem, there were nine, 50+ HR performances, a rate of one every 1.3 years. Indeed, if we expand the analysis to include the entire Steroid Era from 1984, when Jose Canseco said he first started using steroids, to 2002, the last season before MLB began testing for steroids, there were 19, 50+ home run performances, a rate of one every season. Following the introduction of steroid testing (2003-2022) there were 11 more 50 run performances. The pace has slowed to one ever 1.6 seasons.
- Selig's reference to finally becoming concerned about the potential problem of steroids in baseball happening on a Sunday morning in 1998 is from an Associated Press article written by Steve Wilstein on August 21st, 1998. While interviewing McGwire at his locker, Wilstein describes seeing a bottle of Androstenedione (Andro) sitting in plain sight. Andro is a precursor for Testosterone. In other words, in the process of making Testosterone from Cholesterol we make Andro during an intermediate step. Taking Andro in relatively large quantities provides more raw material to make additional Testosterone. Although by 1998 Andro had been banned by the NFL, the IOC, and the NCAA, it was

neither banned in baseball nor was it illegal to purchase over the counter. Thus, McGwire didn't feel any need to hide it and it was prominently displayed in his open locker, "*next to a can of Popeye spinach and packs of sugarless gum* [10]." So, how is it that a perfectly legal supplement was the first warning sign that Bud Selig became aware of? Because it was the first time that the business of baseball was threatened. The article caused a brief disruption in the otherwise positive reporting of the events of the summer of 1998, and Selig couldn't have anything derail the MLB gravy train.

But of all the unbelievable statements in the one paragraph that I have quoted, the most galling was Selig's claim that the reason he was unaware of a steroid problem in baseball was because no one told him there was one. What a remarkably pathetic attempt to deflect responsibility away from himself as the chief executive. However, for the sake of argument, let's assume that Bud Selig and everyone else in the league management office had spent the first six years of the Selig tenure as Commissioner living in a cave on Mars with their eyes closed and their fingers in their ears, and they were completely unaware of the offensive explosion that was happening under their noses. Even then, there was still one way to see that there was something different about these players compared to the 100 years' worth of their predecessors. Just look at them! Over the course of a decade, many baseball players had transformed from having very average looking bodies to being built like linebackers. Take the three most prominent players of the era who we now know took steroids, Sammy Sosa, Mark McGwire, and Barry Bonds. Do a Google search and compare images from before they were confirmed to have started steroids to what they looked like when they were rewriting the record books. Sosa and

Bonds in particular, went from lanky to thick men with massive forearms and tree trunks for legs.

I won't go so far as to call anyone a liar in this book. It is unlikely that Selig had direct evidence on any one player taking steroids during his tenure. But I do believe that he, and many other people in positions of power suspected that steroids had become a prominent part of the game by the early 1990s. If not, why did Selig's predecessor feel it necessary to ban the possession the use of steroids in 1991, just one year before Selig took the helm? What is obvious to me is that the home run record chase of 1998, and the huge increase in home run hitting that preceded it, were both good for the business of baseball, if not for the integrity of the sport itself.

To be sure, the resuscitation of baseball in 1998 would not have happened without steroids. There are two lines of evidence to support this position. First, neither Sosa nor McGwire hit anywhere close to 61 homes runs in a season before they started using steroids. McGwire admits to using steroids regularly throughout the 1990s starting in 1993 while trying to recover from a series of injuries [11]. This period includes the 1998 and 1999 seasons when he hit 70 and 65 home runs respectively. Prior to that his career high for home runs was 49 during his rookie season in 1987. Although Sosa has steadfastly denied having ever used steroids, it was reported by the *New York Times* in 2003 that he was one of 104 players who tested positive in 2002 [12]. But, by looking at changes in his body over the years he appears to add significant bulk between 1996 and 1998. Prior to the 1998 season, Sosa's career best was 36 home runs in 1995. Barry Bonds started using steroids sometime between 1998 and 1999 [7]. Prior to his record-breaking season of 2001 when he hit 73 homers, his best performance was 46 in 1993. If we eliminate all three of these men from the record books, it wouldn't be until 2022 that Maris' record was finally broken by who everyone believes to be a legitimate, non-PED using player, Aaron Judge of the Yankees. Just like we saw prior to the Steroid Era, he only improved on Maris' mark by one home run, hitting his 62nd of the season during the 161st game, 24 years after the summer of McGwire and Sosa.

But even if we establish that the wonderful events of 1998 would not have happened without steroids, many critics insist that the stain placed on the game negates all the benefits that were derived. Baseball fans were defrauded by greedy cheaters, the game and its records were cheapened, and worst of all, the poor, poor children were provided a terrible lesson that taking steroids is the only way to succeed.

Although I'm sure that many fans were offended by the revelation that Sosa and McGwire were juiced, that didn't keep them from spinning the turnstiles. Excluding the Covid-shortened years of 2020 and 2021, attendance has never dipped close the nadir of 1995 (25,021), and between 1999-2022 averaged 29,872 fans per game (Appendix II). As for the game of baseball, besides a brief lockout in 2021 that didn't result in any lost games, baseball has experienced a long stretch of relative peace in labor-management relations. Between 2001 and 2019, the MLB has garnered steady increases in total revenue from 3.58 billion to 10.37 billion over that time, with no decrease in any year other than those affected by Covid [13].

Then there is the issue of the records themselves. If the management of baseball was so incensed by the cheating that tainted their game, it would only make sense that they would expunge the records set by the known cheaters and return them to their rightful owners. But of course, they didn't do that. The record for home runs in a season still belongs to Barry Bonds. To add even more hypocrisy to the already ludicrous self-righteousness of MLB, four years after it became known that Bonds had used steroids during the 2001 season when he broke McGwire's record, he broke the record for most home runs in a career, passing both Babe Ruth and Hank Aaron on the way. That record still stands too. I guess baseball is fine with steroids when they serve their purposes.

This brings us to the purported reason for the Congressional hearings of 2005 and 2007, the children. Of course, I agree that preventing children from taking performance enhancing drugs, particularly steroids and human growth hormone is important, but I chafe at the idea that this is the responsibility of the players. I have a 12-year-old daughter. It is the responsibility of my wife and I to raise her correctly and make sure that she doesn't decide to take PED. We do not abdicate this responsibility to anyone else, least of all professional athletes. The notion of role models has never resonated with me. I was an athlete as a child and young adult. A pretty good one. I never did anything that I thought my favorite athletes were doing just because they were doing it. If I chose to take a supplement or buy a piece of equipment it was because I had researched it and made a conscious decision for which I, and no one else, was responsible.

Why is this emphasis put so specifically on steroids? The National Institutes of Health estimates that each year around 3600 children and young adults under the age of 21 die from alcohol use, in motor vehicle accidents, homicides, suicides, or other alcohol-related incidents [14]. This doesn't stop the endorsement of alcohol by current and former athletes, and other celebrities, and it shouldn't. By contrast, between 1990 and 2012 there was only one documented death resulting from steroid use in the same age group [15]. That's a difference of 262%, but I bet there will never be any Congressional hearings on the use of alcohol in baseball. Did the public outcry make a difference? A study published in 1989 out of the University of Arkansas Medical School reported that an average of 11% of high school students surveyed had used, or were using anabolic steroids [16]. Another study published in 2013 by the MetLife Foundation found that 11% of teens surveyed had used or were using Human Growth Hormone [17]. So, what's changed? It's extremely difficult, and in most cases impossible, to legislate or shame your way to changing human behavior.

Although there are numerous examples of baseball players using steroids and HGH to speed recovery from injury, most of the known cases were for performance enhancement via added muscle mass. When players break the rules, they risk the consequences of suspension, lifetime banishment, loss of income, and public scrutiny. But when the governing body benefits from, and in no small part, enables the cheating, I find it nauseating when the only people punished are the athletes. As you read this, ask yourself what you would do if your boss gave you a subtle wink-wink, as you took PED to improve your job performance. Add on the potential that you might lose that job if your performance slipped. You have no other job skills that will allow you to change careers. Now, let's add in the fact that you grew up destitute in the Dominican Republic. Those drugs allowed you to lift yourself and your family out of crushing poverty. Would you say no? I wouldn't.

My favorite example of how the MLB embraced the steroid-fueled home run era was a Nike commercial that aired at the start of the 1999 season, the better part of a year after Bud Selig thought there might be an issue with steroids in baseball. The scene opens with McGwire taking batting practice with a crowd of adoring fans, including actress Heather Locklair in the stands. The Cardinals' opponent that day is the Atlanta Braves, whose star pitchers Tom Glavine and Greg Maddux become jealous of all the attention McGwire is still attracting a year after breaking the record. On the spot they decide that they need to be hitting home runs too. They start by buying the right shoes, Nikes of course, and then putting themselves through a Rocky-like training montage. Having honed their home run hitting skills they return to the batting cages to show off for Locklair and a smaller audience of attractive young women. Locklair, appearing impressed by their newfound hitting prowess says,

"*Hi Tom.*" Glavine and Maddux do McGwire's signature forearm to forearm bash and Glavine says, "*Chicks dig the long ball.*" But then Locklair asks if they've seen Mark.

It's a funny commercial. I still get a laugh out of it. But in writing this book, there is one short clip in the commercial that didn't register with me in 1999, but now seems telling. The two Cy Young winning pitchers are sitting in a steam room after a training session and Glavine asks Maddux, "*Feel bigger?*" Maddux takes a quick glance at his flexed bicep, "*Yeah.*" And that's what it was, and still is, all about, getting bigger. Size matters in all sports. The size of the athlete, how hard they hit the ball, the number of home runs they can pound over the fence. It all comes down to size. The players were sent a very clear message, get bigger. They did, and everyone was rewarded for it. But when it came time to pay the piper, only the players were asked to pony up. If the owners and management hadn't been threatened by Congressional legislation to manage the steroid problem in baseball, the train would have kept on rolling. To the fans who felt betrayed by the players, as though they had fixed the games and defrauded them of their ticket prices, I say you should have been paying closer attention. Unlike with cycling where steroids are used entirely for their recuperative powers and not to add muscle, in baseball steroids are taken primarily for their anabolic properties. All you had to do was open your eyes. For the less observant, more casual fan, sports is entertainment. The players took a calculated risk to their health, and their freedom to be able to play better and entertain more. It seems remarkably disingenuous to have them be the only people held responsible for the outcome of the decisions that we all made.

Reference:

1. Forman, S. *Baseball Reference*. 2000-2023; Available from: https://www.baseball-reference.com/leagues/majors/misc.shtml.
2. Rains, R., *Mark McGwire: Home Run Hero*. 2011, New York, New York, USA: St. Martin's Press.
3. Sammy Sosa, M.B., *Sammy Sosa: An Autobiography*. 2000, New York, New York, USA: Grand Central Publishing.
4. Sandomir, R., *BASEBALL; Also King of Ratings and the T-Shirts*, in *New York Times*. 1998, The New York Times Company: New York, New York, USA.
5. Tom Clavin, D.P., *Roger Maris: Baseball's Reluctant Hero*. 2011, New York, New York, USA: Simon & Schuster.
6. Lennon, W. *30 for 30*. Long Gone Summer. [8]. A. Schnack. ESPN. 2020.
7. Mark Fainaru-Wada, L.W., *Game of Shadows*. 2006, Sheridan, Wyoming, USA: Gotham Books.
8. Canseco, J., *Juiced*. 2006, New York, New York, USA: Harper Collins.
9. Mitchell, G.J., *REPORT TO THE COMMISSIONER OF BASEBALL OF AN INDEPENDENT INVESTIGATION INTO THE ILLEGAL USE OF STEROIDS AND OTHER PERFORMANCE ENHANCING SUBSTANCES BY PLAYERS IN MAJOR LEAGUE BASEBALL*. 2007, Office of the Commissioner of Baseball. p. 409.
10. Wilstein, S., *Andro' OK in baseball, not Olympics.*, in *Associated Press*. 1998, Associated Press: New York, New York, USA.
11. Kepner, T., *McGwire Admits That He Used Steroids*, in *New York Times*. 2010, The New York Times Company: New York, New York, USA.

12. Schmidt, M.S., *Sosa Is Said to Have Tested Positive in 2003*, in *New York Times*. 2009, The New York Times Company: New York, New York, USA.
13. Statista. *Major League Baseball total league revenue from 2001 to 2022*. 2001-2022; Available from: https://www.statista.com/statistics/193466/total-league-revenue-of-the-mlb-since-2005/.
14. Health, N.I.o., *Alcohol's Effects on Health*, N.I.o.A.A.a. Alcoholism, Editor. 2023, National Institutes of Health: Bethesda, Maryland, USA.
15. Paola Frati, F.P.B., Luigi Cipolloni, Enrico De Dominicis, and Vittorio Fineschi, *Anabolic Androgenic Steroid (AAS) Related Deaths: Autoptic, Histopathological and Toxicological Findings*. Current Neuropharmacology, 2015. **13**: p. 146-159.
16. Mimi D. Johnson, S.J., Brad Shoup, and Vaughn I. Rickert, *Anabolic Steroid Use by Male Adolescents*. Pediatrics, 1989. **83**(6): p. 921-924.
17. Foundation, M., *The Partnership: Attitude Tracking Study*, in *Paternership for Drug-Free Kids*. 2013.

Chapter 6. Good Pitching Will Always Stop Good Hitting and Vice-Versa

"If you know how to cheat, start now." ***—Earl Weaver***

Throughout my elementary and middle school years I attended a series of Montessori schools, the last of which being the Post Oak School in Bellaire, Texas, a small independent city inside of Houston. Although I credit my Montessori education with helping me develop the mind of a free thinker, the one word that I would use to describe my time in the three Montessori schools I attended is *small.* The schools were so very small. My 8th grade class had no more than ten students and I think I may be overestimating that number. Besides a co-ed soccer team that we formed during only my 7th grade year that played against other small private schools, we had no athletics to speak of. When it came time to go to high school there was no thought of sending me to another small private school. I wanted out!

My freshman year at Bellaire High School started in the fall of 1988. Going from a school of around 120 students ranging in age from newborns to 14 years, to a school of over 3500 teenagers was a pleasant shock to the system. I loved being in a public high school. First and foremost, I loved being in a school with around 1700 young women. Going to school with the same 5-10 girls for the prior ten years got to be really boring. I was suddenly surrounded by so many girls that I couldn't pay attention in class and my grades took a brief dip. But, after a few stern talks from my parents, I was able to right the ship.

Beyond the distractions of the opposite sex, there were several simpler oddities that came along with attending a public high school. I loved how big everything was. It was a challenge to get from the third floor of the main building to the temporary shacks on the other side of the campus within the seven minutes allotted between classes. I loved that we had vocational classes like woodwork, metal shop, and auto body repair. I loved home economics where in addition to learning how to reconcile a checkbook and fill out a 1040, I learned how to bake a cake and make beef Wellington. I loved when our school hosted an annual Future Farmers of America day when all the students who were studying agriculture and were destined to attend either Texas A&M or Texas Tech would bring their prized goats, lambs, hogs, rabbits, broilers (chickens), and steer to school to auction them and compete for college scholarships. Of course, more important than the livestock, which were quite impressive, was the BBQ we had those days. But, without question, the most important part of attending a large public high school was the athletic opportunities it provided me, both as a fan and an athlete.

One of the many things that I love about my state is how much emphasis we place on being the biggest and the best. It comes through in all aspects of life, both good and bad. Houston is home to the biggest, most advanced medical center in the world, a place where I spent three years completing my post-doc. Ironically, we also have the most uninsured citizens of any state. But back to the positives: We have some of the best universities and research institutions anywhere in the world. All five of our largest cities, Houston, San Antonio, Austin, Dallas, and Fort Worth, host vibrant, well-funded, well-attended arts scenes. And, of course, we take our sports very, very seriously. Although all five of the big sports, Football, Baseball, Basketball, Hockey, and Soccer are competed at the major league level, in Texas, starting in high school, football is king. Unfortunately for me, Bellaire High School has never been particularly good at football. During my four years between 1988 and 1992, our football team went 10-29-1 with our best season coming during my junior year when we went 5-5. But all schools are good at something and for Bellaire High School that something was baseball. My alma mater has won seven state titles in baseball. We have produced several major league players with the most famous being Chuck Knoblauch (class of 1986) who won four World Series rings with the Minnesota Twins (1991) and the New York Yankees (1998-2000).

As a freshman I was more interested in the spectacle of the game. Even though our fans had to travel across town for all our games because we didn't have a playing field on campus, we packed the house for most games. After reaching the third round of the playoffs my freshman year, I started paying attention to the other schools in the area and their best players. I would stay up to watch the evening news so that I could catch the local sportscasters talk about high school sporting events from across the state. They would regularly highlight one or two players for their athletic (always) and academic (sometimes) abilities. It was during my sophomore year that I first heard about a pitcher from Deer Park High School in Deer Park, Texas, a refinery town about 25 southeast of Houston. Andy Pettitte was a tall lefty who had a complete arsenal of pitches, the best of which was his cutter (also called a slider) that would break late and in on right-handed hitters.

When the bracket for the playoffs came out at the end of the 1990 season, the first team that I looked for was Deer Park. They were in our half of the regional bracket, which meant that if we both got that far, we would meet in the third round. Since we were the higher seed, we had home field advantage in the best-of-three series, hosting games one, and assuming it wasn't a sweep, three. Pettitte was the starting pitcher for Deer Park in the first game. He gave up three hits and struck out 15 batters [1]. I had seen pitchers with more speed who could overpower our hitters, but I hadn't seen a pitcher with so much command of the ball. It was like he had attached a string to the ball that he could yank at the last minute to make the ball cut sideways or dive into the dirt. Now you see the ball, now you don't.

In addition to his cutter, he had an excellent curve, a decent fastball, and a pitch that I had never seen before, a knuckle ball. Unlike his curve and cutter, which required enormous amounts of spin to be put on the ball to make it break either side-to-side or to drop, Pettitte's knuckle ball barely rotated as it travelled through the air. Of the three hitters who faced his knuckleball that day, two were confused by what they saw and froze in place for a strike; the last swung too early and had to watch the ball float by him. Although our pitcher, Kelly Wunsch, who went on to play the better part of five MLB seasons, had a pretty good day on the mound, Pettitte dominated my Cardinals in game one of the series, beating us 4-1. I remember the feeling of the crowd while leaving the stands: we weren't coming back for game three. As good as we were, Deer Park and Andy Pettitte were better. They beat us 6-1 in the second game and went all the way to the state final, losing to Duncanville 6-5.

This was the first time that I had ever paid attention to how a pitcher could manipulate a ball, and by extension opposing batters. The only time prior to this that I had watched any baseball was when the Astros had lost to the New York Mets in six games in the National League Championship Series in 1986. But at 12 years old, and having only followed football and basketball closely, I didn't have a clue what a cutter or a changeup were, and I didn't care. But high school games are different. First, you're closer to the action. If you sit behind home plate at a high school game, you can hear the conversations between catcher, batter, and umpire. If the ball has any movement, you can see it clearly. Second, these were my classmates. I would ask them why they spit into their hand and rubbed it on the ball, and they would ask me why I shaved my legs before a big swim meet. Their answers about baseball were always cooler than anything I could tell them about swimming.

Andy Pettitte fascinated me. Here was a kid, just two years older than me, who was a few years away from playing in the big leagues and he was as accessible to his classmates as our players were to me. Even though he would go on to spend most of his career with the Yankees (whom I hate), winning five World Series titles with the Evil Empire, Pettitte was now one of my favorite players. It helped a lot that he spent three years with the Astros and was part of the 2005 team that took us to our first World Series appearance. His career earned run average (ERA), the number of runs a pitcher is responsible for over a nine-inning game, was a solid 3.8 (Appendix III). His career winning percentage was almost 63%. He won 21 games in a season twice, in 1996 and 2003. More impressive were his post-season stats. He holds three all-time postseason records with 44 starts, 19 wins, and 276 2/3 innings pitched. If not for his brief foray into the realm of PED, many baseball writers think that he would be in the Hall of Fame. I think he should be in regardless.

On December 15th, 2007, I was scrolling through ESPN.com when I saw a headline that caught my attention. Andy Pettitte had admitted to using human growth hormone (HGH) in 2002 [2]. Pettitte had been cited in the Mitchell Report on the use of steroids in baseball and wanted to get out in front of the reporting, apologizing for his *"error in judgement."* At the time he admitted to only receiving two injections from his personal trainer sometime between April 21st and June 14th of that year when he was on the disabled list (DL) with a strained elbow flexor tendon in his pitching arm. But further investigation forced him to concede that he had also received HGH sometime before August of 2004, this time from his father who was taking it illegally in an attempt to recover from an assortment of ailments [3]. In 2004 Pettitte pitched in only 15 games, around half as many as his career average. His previously strained flexor tendon was now torn. Pettitte still insists that his use of HGH in 2004, as in 2002, was a desperate attempt to stay on the active list and stave off surgery until after the season. On August 18th, the Astros shut him down and he prepared to have season-ending surgery a week later.

Recovering from tendon injuries is notoriously difficult. Tendons attach muscles to bones, transmitting enormous amounts of tension from the force-generating muscles to the bones, which serve as levers, allowing us to move our joints. Unlike muscles and bones, tendons are poorly vascularized, meaning that less blood flows through them than through other tissues. When muscles and bones are injured, the already rich blood supply increases dramatically, allowing for the clearance of damaged tissue, and the delivery of raw materials for repair. By contrast, without adequate blood flow tendons rely on swelling of the injured joint to push nutrients into them by diffusion. Depending on the severity of the injury, tendons can heal on their own, but it can take weeks to months before the pain subsides and strength returns to normal. In many cases the tendon never heals completely, and some form of medical intervention is needed. If an elite athlete suffers a torn tendon, either partial or complete, it must be surgically repaired before they can return to their prior form.

So, did Pettitte's claim make scientific sense? Can HGH help heal damaged tendons? Not surprisingly, it's difficult to answer this question directly. The two best studies that I found on the subject were produced by the same lab, with one testing elderly men (65-80 yrs.) [4] and the other young men (20-30 yrs.) [5]. Since finding enough subjects with injuries of similar severity to the same ligament is impractical, both studies used immobilization as a stand-in for injury. When an arm or leg is casted and held in one position for an extended period, the tendons (and muscles) get thinner and weaker, like what happens when you strain a tendon and can't use the muscles attached to it for exercise. Importantly tendons also lose stiffness, meaning that they do not transmit force from the muscles to the bones as well as they did when they were more taught.

Both studies followed a similar design. The subjects were divided into an HGH group which received daily injections for all eight weeks of the study, and a placebo group which received an injection of a non-active substance, likely saline. A cast was placed on a randomly selected leg from the hip to the ankle for two weeks followed by six weeks of resistance training to rehabilitate the muscles and tendons. Regardless of age, casting reduced the stiffness of the Patellar tendon in the placebo group, but not the group that received HGH. After the six weeks of rehabilitation, the thickness of the Patellar tendon also increased more in both the young and elderly HGH groups than in the placebo groups. So, HGH administration prevented atrophy of the Patellar tendon, allowed it to get thicker during rehabilitation, and maintained its stiffness, making it more functional and less susceptible to reinjury.

There you have it: Andy Pettitte was justified in taking HGH, right? Not quite. To the best of our knowledge Pettitte was only administered between two and four injections of HGH in both 2002 and 2004. Each of the subjects in the studies cited were given daily injections for eight weeks (56 injections) of a known concentration and potency. Pettitte got his HGH of unknown concentration, age, storage method, etc. from his personal trainer (2002) and his dad (2004), not the same exacting standards of practice as what was reported in the two well-controlled, peer-reviewed, published studies. Then there is the fact that no amount of HGH is going to fix a torn tendon. Once the structural integrity of the tendon is compromised to that degree, surgery is the only option for repair, particularly for an MLB pitcher who has to repeatedly place his elbow flexor tendon under unusually high strain if he wants to stay on the mound. The data that I've presented suggest that although it's plausible that taking HGH under the supervision of a doctor could speed the recovery from a tendon strain, it's highly unlikely that what most people agree Andy Pettitte did, i.e., taking a few doses of HGH, had any real impact on his rehabilitation. But Andy Pettitte wasn't added to the Mitchel report and issued a congressional subpoena for trying to heal an injury. He isn't in the Hall of Fame because

HGH is considered a performance enhancing drug that tipped the competitive balance in his favor. But did it?

Here I cite a 2008 review paper from Stanford University that included 44 separate studies on the impact of HGH on different measures of athletic performance including aerobic capacity (endurance), anaerobic capacity (strength and power), and body composition [6]. Generally speaking, although HGH did improve body composition a little, it had no impact on strength, power, or endurance. Even the increases in lean mass were likely more attributable to water weight gain than any additional muscle mass. When you add the fact that the HGH groups reported more side effects including edema and water retention, joint pain, and fatigue during exercise, the authors of the review concluded that at best, taking HGH may have allowed for some fat loss, but that it wasn't worth the potential side effects that came with it.

This is solid evidence in support of my contention that Andy Pettitte could not have enhanced his athletic performance by taking HGH while injured in 2002 and 2004, even if he had wanted to. But the best way to answer this question is to look at the data and compare Andy Pettitte's performance during the two years he took HGH, 2002 and 2004, to his historical data, both his career averages and his best years (Appendix III). Between 1995 and 2001, Pettitte pitched in between 31 and 35 games each season. In 2002, injury limited him to 22 games after he returned from the DL in mid-June. In those games he went 13-5 with four no-decisions. That's a winning percentage of 72.2%, which is higher than his career average of 62.6%, but only his fourth best performance. His ERA was 3.27, again better than his career average of 3.8, but also just his fourth best year for his career. In 2004 he started only 15 games before ending his season early in August. But even then, he had a winning percentage of 60% and an ERA of 3.9. What I find more interesting is what happened in the two seasons after Pettitte took HGH, long after any potential benefit would have worn off. In 2003, after a full offseason of rehab and conditioning, Pettitte played in 33 games, and won 21 (tied for his best total). He had a winning percentage of 72.4%, and an ERA of 4.02. In 2004, with a surgically repaired pitching arm, he again played in 33 games and won 17, his fifth best total. But his ERA was 2.39, by far his career best, giving up 1.4 fewer runs per game than his career average.

Is it possible that by taking a few doses of HGH Andy Pettitte was able to maintain his performance well enough to match his usual output in 2002 and 2004? No one can ever know because we can't repeat the conditions as they were without HGH and see what happened. The more important question to ask is whether or not a sustained, doctor-monitored program of HGH injections, in conjunction with traditional rehab methods, would have hastened Pettitte's recovery in 2002? Although I think there is some good data to support this hypothesis, what we currently have is a very squishy *maybe*. What is abundantly clear is that Andy Pettitte's actions did not enhance his performance. So, should he be on the list of players worthy of the Hall of Fame who will never be admitted? That's for each fan to decide for themselves. My position is that he should be a member in good standing. But context matters in these situations. We must know what he was thinking when he made his decisions. Lucky for us Andy Pettitte told us.

> *"In 2004, when I tore the flexor tendon in my pitching arm, I again used HGH two times in one day out of frustration and in a futile attempt to recover. Unfortunately, I needed surgery on the arm later in the year. I regret these lapses in judgment [3]."*

> *"My dad had been using it. He ended up bringing me two syringes over to my house. And you know, I injected myself once in the*

morning and once at night. ... I did it for that day. And to this day, I don't know why... I was desperate and you know I really knew that it wasn't going to help me. My flexor tendon was already torn. I knew I needed surgery. I would just say just out of desperation I tried to do it again. But that was the extent of it [7]."

What would you have done in his shoes? You have a lingering injury to your pitching arm, the one part of your body that you can't work without. The injury won't heal with anything less than surgery that will cost you at least one season. You have teammates and a fan base who are depending on you to get back on the mound. And let's not minimize the monetary factor, although your current contract is guaranteed, your future earnings largely depend on what you do now. The sentiments expressed by Andy Pettitte are visceral and sincere. His desperation is clear. Does this justify his actions? I think that it does. No, he wasn't forced to do anything he didn't ultimately want to do. But it's clear to me that if not for his injury he likely would not have taken HGH. But, even then, did he really break the rules of baseball? Technically, yes. But it's important to remember that although many in baseball leadership insist that HGH was *"banned"* in 1991 when then commissioner Fay Vincent sent a league-wide memo, that he has since described as more of a *"moral statement"* than a *"legal one,"* there was no written rule change that explicitly banned its use until 2011. In an interview with the Sporting News from 2016 [8], Vincent further explained his actions in regard to steroids (and HGH) in 1991.

SPORTING NEWS: *"I know when you were commissioner of baseball you banned steroids, but the players' union didn't agree to testing until 2004. I was curious to get your* *thoughts on players doing better in Hall of Fame voting who may have been steroid users."*

FAY VINCENT: "*Well, you have it wrong. I didn't ban steroids. The Congress of the United States said steroids were on the prohibited substance list. It's a common misunderstanding that steroids were not banned in baseball until much later. They were banned by Congress. What I did was say, 'Because they're banned by Congress, we are gonna be bound by those restrictions, and steroids are gonna be a problem.'"*

"So, yes I put out a memo in 1990 or '91 saying, 'Because Congress has put steroids on the prohibited substance list, you ought to be aware that for people in baseball who are not subject to the union's authority, I'm going to treat steroids as a serious matter.'"

What?! Let's analyze that last statement. *"for people in baseball who are not subject to the union's authority, I'm going to treat steroids as a serious matter."* The only people in baseball **not** subject to the authority of the player's union is everyone **EXCEPT** the players. Good thing the Commissioner's office took such a tough stance on the use of steroids by the janitors and concessionaires of baseball. But seriously, the commissioner of the sport stated in 2016 that he indeed **DID NOT** ban steroids, but he would be very grumpy if he found out (not sure how exactly, since testing didn't start until 2004) that any players were taking these drugs. Putting aside the *"moral memo,"* baseball did not enact any written rule changes that explicitly banned steroids until 2005, and HGH until 2011.

So, let's summarize. Although Major League Baseball said in 1991 that using HGH was frowned upon, they did not put this in the rule book for another 20 years. That means that when Andy Pettitte injected himself with HGH in 2002 and 2004 in two futile attempts to heal an injury so he could get back to work, he wasn't breaking any rules. Thus, what he did, although maybe immoral according to Fay Vincent's definition, was not cheating. Period. By referencing his stats during those times it's possible, but unlikely that Pettitte's use of HGH allowed him to limp along better than he would have otherwise, but it was clearly not performance enhancing. So, what would you have done under those circumstances? I would probably have pull down my pants and let my personal trainer give me a jab of HGH in the butt and hope for the best.

Anecdotally, these results match what athletes and coaches have said about HGH for years. By itself HGH does little to enhance performance. Instead, what it does is allow for faster recovery between bouts of exercise, allowing for restoration and healing of injured muscles, bones, and tendons. The reason HGH is often taken with steroids is because anabolic agents like steroids accelerate muscle growth beyond the rate at which the other connective tissues, i.e., bones, ligaments, cartilage, and most often, tendons can keep up. You end up with unnaturally large muscles pulling on tendons that are not equal to the task. The weakest link fails, leaving athletes with strained, torn, and ruptured tendons.

But all this can also happen while training without doping. Any periodized training routine, be it aerobic endurance training or strength training, will start with a period of a few weeks to months of gradually increasing load that those who taught me referred to as the anatomical adaptation phase. If you skip this phase and start lifting heavy weights immediately, the muscles will adapt to the additional load and grow at a pace too fast for the tendons. The result is a lot of injured athletes.

During the offseason and preseason, coaches have plenty of time to allow their athletes to recover between training sessions to allow for the body to repair its muscles and tendons. The levels of HGH and testosterone both spike during and immediately after exercise just for this reason. But once the season starts, there is very little if any time for recovery. Repeated maximal efforts and acute injuries build up. Prolonged stress, both physical and emotional, combined with travel, poor sleep habits, and time away from loved ones leads to significant increases in stress hormones like cortisol, which drive down the production of HGH and testosterone. We now have the perfect recipe for chronic injuries.

There are three obvious remedies to this problem: 1. Reduce the length of the regular season and playoffs in sports (or the severity and length or individual events like the Tour de France). Fewer games reduce the likelihood of injuries. 2. fundamentally change the nature of the most dangerous games, e.g., football, basketball, pitching in baseball, etc., to reduce the likelihood and severity of injuries, or 3. allow athletes to use HGH and other currently banned substances to speed recovery after injury. Of course, this would have to happen under the supervision of a qualified medical professional. Recent developments in football, basketball, and baseball have shown us what ownership thinks of my first two options.

- Starting in 2021 the NFL increased the length of the regular season from 16 to 17 games. They would've gone to 18, but the players' union refused until they could bargain for a bigger cut of the revenue generated by the two extra games. At the same time, they added one more playoff team in each conference to the post-season.
- Prior to the 2020-2021 season, 16 teams qualified for the NBA playoffs each season. For the last three seasons, the four teams sitting in places 7-10 in each conference played anywhere from 1-3 extra games

during a play-in tournament before the playoffs began. Expanding on this model of more games equals more money, the 2023-2024 NBA season will introduce an in-season tournament. For now, only the two teams that make it to the championship will play an extra game. But the history of sports has shown us that if something is successful, i.e., it makes more money for the owners, it will be kept and expanded.

- Baseball has progressively increased the number of teams that make the playoffs from four in the 1980s to eight in 1995, and now 12. Each iteration added more games to be played. Just as we saw when the Tour de France added more and steeper mountain passes to satisfy the desires of the fans, a longer regular and post-season keeps more fans engaged, i.e., spending money. But the more we ask of athletes, the more frequent and severe the injuries that they experience.
- Of greatest concern is the expansion of the College Football Playoff. Currently four teams qualify for the playoff after a 12-13 game regular season. In most instances the national champion plays 15 games. Starting in 2024 the playoffs will expand to include 12 teams, meaning that the winner will play 4-5 more games after the 12-13 game regular season. That's a total of 16-18 games, which seems excessive for amateur athletes in a collision sport like football. But hey, money talks.

So, since we should only expect the management of professional sports leagues and events to expand their product, player safety be damned, why not consider allowing for the monitored and controlled use of substances that science has shown can help speed recovery? This won't be doping because it won't be done for the purpose of performance enhancement. Because of the federal laws that prohibit the use of anabolic steroids and HGH for anything other than a strictly defined set of ailments, my proposal cannot be undertaken. But that's why I'm writing this book, to try and change minds using empirical data and logic. I am not the first to propose this change in our perception of these drugs and practices. As a matter of fact, this very point was made during the congressional hearings on the use of steroids in baseball in 2008. The player's union Executive Director Donald Fehr hypothesized about this during his testimony.

> *"The last thing I'll say, and I want to stress that I am saying this because I'm musing a bit in response to your question. I am not saying it because it represents a position of the Players Association or even one that I advocate. But I have wondered given the anecdotal suggestion about ability to recover better if some of these things are used* [steroids and HGH], *whether in fact there are therapeutic doses which could be administered to people who have--elderly people with broken hips. I mentioned that because we had an experience in my family with that recently. That would be helpful, and I don't know whether any of that research has been done. But that's a musing on my part."* ***Donald Fehr***

Reference:

1. McMurray, B., *Deer Park Takes Lead on Bellaire*, in *Houston Chronicle*. 1990, Hearst Newspapers LLC: New York, New York, USA.
2. Press, A. *Pettitte Admits Using HGH to Recover From an Elbow Injury in 2002*. ESPN.com 2007.
3. Pettitte, A., *AFFIDAVIT OF ANDY PETTITTE*. 2008.
4. A. P. Boesen, K.D., C. Couppé, S. P. Magnusson, P. Schjerling, M. Boesen, P. Aagaard, M. Kjaer, and H. Langberg, *Effect of growth hormone on aging connective tissue in muscle and tendon: gene expression, morphology, and function following immobilization and rehabilitation*. Journal of Applied Physiology, 2014. **116**: p. 192-203.
5. A. P. Boesen, K.D., C. Couppe, S. P. Magnusson, P. Schjerling, M. Boesen, M. Kjaer and H. Langberg, *Tendon and skeletal muscle matrix gene expression and functional responses to immobilisation and rehabilitation in young males: effect of growth hormone administration*. Journal of Physiology, 2013. **591**(23): p. 6039-6052.
6. Hau Liu, D.M.B., Ingram Olkin, Anne and V.L. Friedlander, Brian Roberts, Eran Bendavid, Olga Saynina, Shelley R. Salpeter, Alan M. Garber, andAndrew R. Hoffman, *Systematic Review: The Effects of Growth Hormone on Athletic Performance*. Annals of Internal Medicine, 2008. **20**(10): p. 747-758.
7. Press, A. *Pettitte Says he Used HGH Supplied by Father in 2004*. ESPN.com 2008.
8. Womack, G. *Former MLB Commissioner Fay Vincent Talks PEDs, Buck O'Neil, Gambling*. Sporting News, 2016.

Chapter 7. What's Good for the Goose...

"The mind has to wrap around... the foot." ***—Michael Scott, Dunder Mifflin Paper***

The 2018 Houston Astros won a then franchise record 103 games and finished first in the AL West division by six games. Coming off our first World Series championship the previous season, they were the prohibitive favorites to win it again, and the postseason campaign started as I had expected when they dispatched with the Cleveland Indians with a 3-0 sweep in the AL Divisional Series, and then opened the ALCS with a road win in Boston. But then the wheels fell off the bus and we lost four straight to the eventual champion Red Sox. I couldn't tell if this sudden change in fortune was a harbinger of more losing seasons to come or just a brief interruption in our winning ways. But by the midpoint of the 2019 season, it was clear that the Astros had a lot more winning to do.

We finished the regular season with a league-best, and new team record, 107 wins. After getting passed the Tampa Bay Rays in the ALDS, we beat the Yankees in dramatic fashion with a game six walk-off home run from Jose Altuve. Our opponent in the World Series was the Washington Nationals who finished second in their division with 14 fewer wins than Houston. Although the Astros were the heavy betting favorite, I was uneasy about the Nationals. They had beaten the 106-win Dodgers in the NLDS, taking the deciding fifth game in extra innings at Dodger stadium, and then mauled the St. Louis Cardinals in a four-game sweep in the ALCS. The Nationals were hot and playing with house money. Unlike the Astros who had won a championship and made another deep run in the playoffs in the previous two seasons, few people expected much from the Nationals.

In all major team sports, while a good offense will fill the stands, if you expect to win a championship, you had better have a solid defense. In baseball, this means that you need great pitching. The 2019 World Series was a duel between two excellent pitching staffs. The Astros were led by Justin Verlander, Gerrit Cole, and Zack Grienke while the Nationals had Stephen Strasburg and Max Sherzer. The first two games in Houston went to the road team with Sherzer getting the better of Cole in game one and Strasburg beating Verlander in game two. Understandably, most Houstonians, including myself, were concerned that the series wouldn't return to the Bayou City. But our second-line pitchers came through in games three and four tying the series at two games apiece heading into game five when the rematch of Cole and Sherzer was scheduled to take place on October 27th. This is where the story became relevant to this book.

On the morning of the game Max Sherzer woke up with a shooting pain radiating from the right side of his neck down his right, pitching arm. The pain was so intense that he couldn't lift his arm. He was diagnosed with an inflamed disc between his fifth and sixth cervical vertebrae. The bulging disc was pinching the fifth and sixth cervical nerves that direct movement in the upper arm (5th), and forearm and hand (6th). Sherzer was quickly scratched for game five, but the next question became whether or not he could recover in time to return to the lineup in either game six or seven. His treatment started with a cortisone injection in his neck at the level of the C5-C6 joint.

Like testosterone, cortisone is a steroid hormone, but without any anabolic properties, in other words, cortisone doesn't stimulate muscle growth. Instead, cortisone reduces inflammation, i.e., the body's way of directing immune cells to an area of tissue damage or infection. Because Sherzer had a long history of neck spasms prior to this episode, it's likely that the inflammation in his neck was caused by the extreme nature of his pitching motion and too little recovery. His injured vertebral disc began leaking debris into his circulation that activated his immune system to send in white blood cells (WBC) to remove the damaged tissue. Before the advent of cortisone and other synthetic anti-inflammatory steroid hormones, the typical course of treatment for this kind of injury would include numbing the pain with any assortment of over the counter or prescription pain pills, icing the area to reduce blood flow and swelling, and waiting for it to heal. Although most people associate the pain experienced after an injury as little more than a nuisance, pain plays the key role of signaling that something is injured, and that further use may cause additional, possibly irreparable damage. But Scherzer didn't have time to wait for his neck to heal on its own. The Nationals needed him back in the rotation as quickly as possible, hopefully for game seven, assuming the Nationals could get that far. Without him on the mound, the Astros won game five and were heading back to Texas with a 3-2 series lead.

For the next 24 hours after his injection, Scherzer wore a neck brace and rested as best he could. Then the team chiropractor took over and worked to reduce the swelling and improve the mobility of his neck and shoulder. Because the Astros didn't close the series in game six, amazingly Sherzer got his chance to start in a winner-take-all game seven. He pitched five solid innings, giving up only five hits and two runs. The Nationals beat us 6-2 to win their first World Series. It was the first time that I had ever seen a series in which every game was won by the road team. To this day I don't think the Nationals would have won without Scherzer starting game seven. If not for that cortisone injection, Max Scherzer doesn't pitch in game seven and the Astros win their second title in three seasons. But here's the rub: if this same scenario were to have happened in cycling, and Max Sherzer needed a cortisone injection in his neck or any other part of his body to get on his bike and compete, he would be disqualified and subject to an extended competition ban of up to two years for a first offense. There are a several recent examples of this disparity in how different sports legislate the use of pain-relieving drugs. Before I get into that, I need to explain why cortisone is on the banned list for at least some sports.

Cortisone is one of a group of synthetic steroid hormones called corticosteroids that are taken to reduce inflammation. There are several related corticosteroids with similar properties that you may have heard of, for example prednisone, prednisolone, dexamethasone, and hydrocortisone are common examples. These drugs can be delivered as pills, creams, eye drops, inhalers, or injections. As I described above, inflammation is an immune response to injury or infection, and although we want our immune system to respond to these signals of trouble, sometimes that response is misdirected, as with allergies, autoimmune diseases, or they are excessive and prolonged, as with chronic joint injuries. After stepping on a rock while running, I required periodic cortisone injections in my foot until I had the money and time for some reconstructive surgery of my right ankle. Whenever I get the flu or a sinus infection, in addition to antibiotics (for a bacterial infection) I also ask for cortisone, either by injection or pill. My immune system goes crazy when I get sick, causing my symptoms to be quite severe and prolonged. Controlling the immune response to infection and illness in many instances actually speeds the recovery process because it brings the immune system back under control. But *"control"* really means suppression of the immune system, and if you take it too far you leave yourself open to infection.

Participation in athletics causes inflammation. There is more than a nugget of truth in the old adage, *"No pain, no gain."* For example, strength training makes your muscles undergo hypertrophy, i.e., they get bigger. But for your muscles to hypertrophy they must be subjected to external loads big enough to cause small tears to form. As with Max Sherzer's neck, the damage causes an inflammatory response. The muscles swell with fluid carrying WBC that clear the damaged tissue, and nutrients to make new muscle tissue.

The inflammation causes pain that peaks between 48 and 72 hours after the workout. It hurts when you poke the muscles or try to move them. This is called delayed-onset muscle soreness or DOMS, and although there are training methods that can reduce its duration and severity, DOMS is an unavoidable part of getting bigger and faster. Taking cortisone in response to DOMS impairs hypertrophy, so no informed athlete would take it for this kind of expected and controlled injury.

Cortisone is more likely to be used in-season in response to an acute or chronic injury when there is not time for adequate recovery before the next competition. For example, the 2023 Tour de France covered a distance of 2116 miles in 23 days, 21 days of racing and two rest days. That's an average of 100 miles a day, much of it raced at the cyclists' physiological limit. Aside from the obvious injuries that occur after crashes, e.g., broken bones, sprained joints, bruises, concussions, and road rash, cyclists often suffer from an assortment of more mundane injuries that make riding a bike painful, including knee tendonitis, chronic pain of the neck, back, shoulders, hands, and feet, and the one injury to rule them all, saddle sores. A saddle sore is a puss-filled abscess or open, oozing lesion often on the peritoneum, the space between the anus and scrotum (or labia). Doesn't that sound fun? Once a saddle-sore opens there's no closing it without getting off the bike for several days. But if caught early a saddle sore can be effectively treated with a topical corticosteroid. Until 2022, cyclists were still allowed to use some corticosteroids in competition if they had a therapeutic use exemption.

So why are cortisone and other related anti-inflammatory steroids on the banned list for some sports if they have such an obvious therapeutic benefit to injured athletes? Quite simply, when taken in doses well above what most doctors would prescribe, they make you feel like Superman. Corticosteroids are potent stimulators of the central and peripheral nervous systems. If you have ever been prescribed a blister pack of steroids as part of your treatment for a respiratory infection, you may have experienced a dramatic improvement of your symptoms within a few hours of taking your first dose. The fog lifts, you can think, the general ickiness and fatigue abate, and you feel at least somewhat normal. Putting this into the context of cycling, or any other sport, cortisone heightens awareness and reduces the sensations of fatigue and pain.

Most of the research on the impact of corticosteroids on athletic performance clearly shows a significant effect. In a 2007 study ten moderately fit young men were given either prednisolone or a placebo for seven days and then asked to ride to exhaustion at 70-75% of their maximum aerobic intensity [1]. On average, a week of corticosteroids improved their time to exhaustion from 46.1 minutes to 74.5. That's a very big increase in time to exhaustion. Even when accounting for the fact that these were not elite athletes dealing with heat, wind, mountains, unruly fans, and team tactics, this is still an impressive outcome that speaks to why, when used improperly, corticosteroids are PED.

So, is it possible that Max Scherzer's game seven heroics in the 2019 World Series were the result of the cortisone injection he received three days prior, i.e., was he doped? It's highly unlikely. First, when received as an injection into a muscle or joint, cortisone is released more slowly than it is when taken in pill form or intravenously, which is how cyclists would take it when doping. When corticosteroids are administered intravenously or orally, the circulating levels peak quickly, between 30-90 min, compared to 24 hours when taken by injection, and the peak circulating concentration is 200-300X higher [2, 3]. Thus, most of the cortisone that he received stayed at the site of his injury (his neck) and didn't leak into his circulation to stimulate his nervous system. Combined with the 72-hour lag period between injection and competition, and whatever cortisone made it into his circulation was likely metabolized and washed out by the time Scherzer took the mound. Finally, there is the matter of dosage. In the study that I cited above [1], the subjects received 60 mg/day of prednisone for a week before they were tested for their time to exhaustion. Of course, we don't know how much cortisone Scherzer received, but the typical dosage for an injection to relieve joint pain is between 20-80 mg. I have received injections in both feet (20 mg each time), my left knee (50 mg), and right shoulder (25 mg), all much less than what was given the subjects in the cycling study.

But, as always, the best way to answer this question is to look at his performance data (Table 4). In game seven, Scherzer pitched five innings and gave up two earned runs for an ERA of 2.4. His ERA for the 2019 regular season was 2.92 and he averaged 6 1/3 innings pitched per game. For the 2019 postseason his ERA was 2.4 while pitching five innings per game. Finally, his game one performance, before he was injured and received his cortisone injection, was the same as what he did throughout the postseason and in game seven, namely an ERA of 2.4 on five innings of pitching. Clearly, there was no performance enhancement. Even if we bring in his career stats as they stand on the day that I am writing this chapter (ERA 3.15 on an average of 6 2/3 innings per game), it's clear that Scherzer's numbers were as steady as a rock.

Table 4. Max Scherzer's Statistics for his Career, the 2019 Regular and Post-Seasons (PS), and During Games 1 and 7 of the World Series.

Career ERA	Career IP	2019 ERA	2019 IP	2019 PS ERA	2019 PS IP	Game 1 ERA	Game 1 IP	Game 7 ERA	Game 7 IP
3.15	6.2	2.92	6.4	2.4	5	2.16	5	2.4	5

ERA = Earned Run Average defined as the number of runs that the pitcher is responsible per nine inning game.
IP = Inning Pitched per game.

In this case the doctor-administered cortisone made it so that an athlete could play through an injury, as was his want, and perform at his usual level, not worse, but certainly not better. This is the same as I would expect for any hard-working man or woman dealing with a lingering injury who still needs to go to the office or pick up their kids. But, if Max Scherzer were a cyclist in the Tour de France nursing an acute injury after a fall, and he received a shot of cortisone from the team doctor, he would be disqualified, subject to a lengthy suspension, and the target of scorn. Instead, Scherzer was hailed as a tough, gritty hero who played through the pain of injury to help his team win a championship. You would expect that with such a disparity between sports, at some point, someone in cycling would point out the double standard. That's exactly what happened a few years later, in the most fitting of locations, France.

The four major tennis tournaments are played on three different surfaces. The US and Australian Opens are played on hard court, Wimbledon is played on grass, and the French Open in played on clay. Each surface has different characteristics that favor certain types of players. Grass, being the fastest surface, favors players with big serves who employ a serve and volley game where they get their opponent out of position with a big serve and then approach the net to cut off the return. Clay, on the other hand, is the slowest surface and is preferred by players who play at the baseline, running side to side, and hitting drop shots with lots of backspin.

Clay court players must be able to sprint and slide to a stop, before changing directions and sprinting the other way. This puts a huge strain on the legs, in particular the feet. The undisputed King of Clay is Spaniard Rafael Nadal. He is one of only eight men with a career grand slam, meaning he has won all four major titles at least once. He has won 22 major singles titles, 14 of them at the French Open. He arrived in Paris for the 2022 tournament with a lingering injury to his left foot caused by a degenerative disease called Mueller-Weiss syndrome, where one of the bones that forms the upper arch of the foot slowly dies because of a lack of blood flow.

Like many degenerative diseases, it may flare unexpectedly causing severe pain, making his sprinting-sliding style of baseline play difficult, if not impossible. Although his diagnosis was made in 2005, he was able to play through the pain until 2021 when he finally had surgery to shore up the failing left foot.

Entering the 2022 French Open, Nadal was in noticeable discomfort, and was seen limping between and during matches. The news quickly spread that to knock down the pain in his foot, Nadal had required an unspecified number of numbing injections and possibly anti-inflammatories during the two-week tournament. Despite the pain and the distractions of his treatment regimen, Nadal won his 14th French Open singles title, losing only three sets during the whole tournament and winning the final in straight sets, 6-3, 6-3, 6-0, a dominant performance under any circumstance. When asked after the tournament about his injections, Nadal wisely offered little detail.

> *"I played without feeling in my foot. I played with an injection in the nerve, and the foot was asleep, that's why I was able to play."* When asked how many injections he required, he coyly answered, *"It's better that you don't know."*

In short order a debate began about the inherent unfairness of what Nadal was allowed to do that other athletes could not. French cyclist, Thibaut Pinot, who had lost the better part of two seasons to back problems stemming from a crash he suffered during the 2020 Tour de France made it clear that although he was not suggesting that Nadal was undeserving of his win, what he did would not be allowed in cycling.

> *"In no case his career or his talent are called into question here. We see too many athletes using this kind of practice in recent weeks. I almost lost two of surely the most beautiful years of my career to take care of my back, it was difficult, but I am proud of it today. The methods [used by Nadal] are simply prohibited in my sport, which is unfortunately so decried."* ***X (Formerly Twitter)***

Fellow Frenchman Guillaume Martin, speaking with the French sports daily *L'Equipe,* shared similar sentiments [4].

> *"What Nadal has done would be impossible in cycling. And I think that's normal. If someone is sick or injured, they don't compete - that seems like common sense to me. First and foremost, for the health of the athletes. I'm not sure the long-term injections will be good for Nadal's foot. In addition, drugs and certainly injections not only have a curative effect, but they can certainly also have an effect on performance or can be used to improve performance. I think that's borderline. If a rider did the same - it's forbidden, but suppose it wasn't - everyone would accuse him [the cyclist] of doping, while they praise Nadal precisely because he can suffer so much pain. The winner in the race, and especially that of the Tour, is systematically accused of doping, even if there is no reason for it at all."*

The Spanish Society of Sports Medicine (SEMED) and the World Anti-Doping Agency (WADA) quickly responded in support of Nadal, stating that numbing injections are not on the prohibited list of substances and thus wouldn't be prohibited in cycling or any other sport that follows WADA rules. But I was unable to find any statement that conclusively stated that Nadal did not also receive corticosteroid injections or pills. Although numbing injections are legal in cycling, cortisone is not. In 2019, the governing body of cycling, the Union Cycliste Internationale (UCI) instituted a rule that any athlete receiving therapeutic corticosteroids to treat an injury or illness would be prohibited from competition for eight days after the last treatment [5]. Interestingly, the UCI, didn't cite as their reason for the ban the potential performance enhancing properties of corticosteroids, but rather the safety of the athletes as *"glucocorticoids can trigger undesirable side-effects which, in the case of an accident or medical emergency, can be life threatening."* More on this is a minute.

Tennis has a long history of allowing corticosteroid use during competitions. Famously, during his farewell tour of tennis during the 2006 US Open, Andre Agassi suffered from back spasms during his second-round match that were so painful he had to lie flat on his back on the concrete while waiting for a car to pick him up and take him to the hospital for a cortisone injection into his lower back to reduce the swelling that was pinching nerves. He lost in four sets in the third round to end his illustrious career.

Even if Nadal had only received anesthetic injections to numb the nerves in his foot, that still carries significant risk. Think about your last trip to the dentist that required numbing your your mouth. How well did your lips and tongue work when you were asked to swish water when it was done? I spit all over myself and the poor hygienist sitting next to me. To be fair the nerves that are numbed for dental procedures have both sensory and motor functions which is why you can't control your lips very well after the injection. The nerves that were numbed in Nadal's foot were likely only the sensory nerves, so controlling movement would not have been directly impaired. That said, not being able to feel your foot, one of two points of contact on the ground as you're trying to run full tilt in one direction, sliding to a stop, and going the other way just as fast. With a numb foot, it's obvious that the risk of further injury is significantly increased.

What if Nadal had pulled a muscle, turned an ankle, ruptured a tendon, how would he have known? The SEMED is correct that any cyclist who wanted an anesthetic injection to numb an injury could technically get one, but what a terrible idea that would be. Does anyone really think that flying down a mountain at 60-80 mph with a numb left foot isn't a risk? Of course not. This cyclist should be kept out of the race because they are not just risking further injury to the foot, if they go down at those speeds, they are risking their lives and the lives of everyone around them, including the support staff and fans on the side of the road.

Remember, pain isn't a nuisance, it's a physiological warning sign that something is wrong and that you should probably stop what you're doing. Regardless of the potential for additional injury, I think that it's the right of each athlete, within reason, to assess how much risk they are willing to take, and to be provided the tools to manage their pain to whatever degree they feel appropriate. But, if the overriding concern about doping is the general health of the athlete, then what's good for the goose has got to be good for the gander. If cortisone injections are considered doping in cycling, the same should apply to tennis and baseball. If anesthetic injections increase the risk of further injury by decreasing proprioception (sensing where you are in space), the practice of numbing athletes should be banned.

So why does cycling treat corticosteroids so differently than do either tennis or baseball? Baseball is easy. Like the other major American sports leagues, i.e., the NFL and NBA, MLB is not a signatory of the WADA anti-doping codes. They have their own list of banned substances, testing protocols and punishments, an innately independent, American approach to the problem. Tennis, however, is governed by WADA rules, which makes their historically lax view on the use of corticosteroids puzzling. An educated guess as to the different approaches between tennis and cycling is related to the historical impact that doping has had on cycling, and not tennis. No sport has as well-documented a history of doping as does cycling.

The earliest iterations of the Tour de France were powered, at least in part, by alcohol, strychnine, and amphetamines, and no one hid it. The heavily publicized scandals on the 1990s and 2000s, that included ghoulish tales of blood bags being delivered in the middle of the night, devastated the sport. Unlike what happened after the Steroid Era of baseball when its popularity only grew, cycling lost a huge segment of its fan base, some of whom have only recently returned. Justifiably, the UCI kicked out its leadership that was either in league with the offenders, or at the very least turned a blind eye as the results of doping grew the sport to a level unimaginable before 1999.

The new regime that came in after Lance Armstrong was exposed brought in new testing protocols and rules to catch dopers and disincentivize cheating with stiffer penalties. But as is usually the case when a pendulum swings from a state of permissiveness to intolerance, it may have swung too far. That said, I'm not the one who has to make the decisions about what are and are not reasonable exceptions for the therapeutic use of substances on the banned list. It's much easier to establish a blanket rule and make everyone abide by it without exception. But there must be a level of consistency between sports that doesn't currently exist. If baseball and tennis can figure out how to allow their injured athletes to be treated with corticosteroids, or any other medicines, while in the care of a medical professional, so can all sports. However, if it is determined that the best course of action is to make all injured athletes sit out training and competition until they've healed, so be it. But let's make the goose sit out like we do the gander.

Reference:

1. Alexandre Arlettaz, H.P., Anne-Marie Lecoq, Natlatie Rieth, Jacques de Ceaurriz, and Katia Collomp, *Effects of Short-Term Prednisolone Intake During Submaximal Exercise.* Medicine & Science in Sports & Exercise, 2007. **39**(9): p. 1672-1678.
2. Caroline Jung, S.G., Hanh HT Nguyen, Jui T Ho, John G Lewis, David J Torpy, and Warrick J Inder, *Plasma, Salivary and Urinary Cortisol Levels Following Physiological and Stress Doses of Hydrocortisone in Nnormal Volunteers.* BMC Endocrine Disorders, 2014. **14**(91).
3. Rozalin R. Dickson, J.M.R., Wayne T. Nicholson, Tim J. Lamer, W. Michael Hooten, *Corticosteroid and Cortisol Serum Levels Following Intra-articular Triamcinolone Acetonide Lumbar Facet Joint Injections.* Pain Practice, 2018. **18**(7): p. 864-870.
4. Roos, A., *Guillaume Martin on Nadal's infiltrations: "I have difficulty understanding"*, in *L'Equipe.* 2022, Éditions Philippe Amaury: Paris, France.
5. (UCI), U.C.I. *The UCI welcomes WADA decision concerning the banning of glucocorticoids.* 2021; Available from: https://www.uci.org/pressrelease/the-uci-welcomes-wada-decision-concerning-the-banning-of-glucocorticoids/TKB8XrVkF4jo4DOZsro7x.

Chapter 8. It's called CANnabis, not CAN'Tabis.

*"That is not a drug, it's a leaf." —**Arnold Schwarzenegger, Governor of California, 2007***

My sister's wedding took place on the Colvos Passage of Puget Sound, west of Vashon Island in 2018. I don't get many chances to go back to the pacific northwest where I went to college, so we decided to pack in some visits with as many old friends as possible. We stayed in Seattle with two of my old college friends and their four kids. After a parents-night-out, my wife and I asked if our hosts would take us to a marijuana dispensary, something we definitely don't have in Texas. Ten minutes later we were looking at an amazing assortment of different products: buds, drinks, candies, gummies, cookies, and brownies. Neither of us enjoys smoking, so edibles were what we wanted. We chose an infused chocolate bar and headed back to our friends' house giggling like teenagers. We had too much to do before the wedding to be high, so we decided that we would wait until after the wedding to partake.

My sister and brother-in-law picked an amazing day without a cloud in the sky. Next to my own wedding, this is still my favorite family event. As we usually do, my wife and I added an athletic event to our trip. We found a 10k to run in Portland that weekend. This would be my daughter's first race at this distance after completing several 5k's. The day after the wedding, we woke up at 4 AM and took an Amtrack from Tacoma to Portland. Coming from Texas, a train trip was a unique experience that we all thoroughly enjoyed. When we arrived in Portland, we had to hustle to the start line before the race set off at 8 AM. Our daughter set the pace, walking when needed. We all finished with smiles, had a couple of hot dogs and beers (not my daughter), and headed back to our AirBnB in downtown Portland and crashed.

That evening, after dinner and an obligatory trip to Voodoo Donuts, we packed our daughter off to sleep and took to the living room with its amazing view of Mount Baker. We quizzed each other on what the dispensary clerk had told us about how much chocolate to eat, and then double checked that by reading the directions on the packaging. My wife, always the more cautious of the two of us, decided to take half the recommended amount. Since I am easily twice her size, I took the full amount. After about an hour the fun began. It had been years since I had partaken of weed and it was a fun trip. Besides all the unstoppable fits of laughter about absolutely nothing, what I remember most is an overwhelming feeling that I was slowly sinking into the floor. My wife quotes me as repeatedly stating that I was *"very heavy"* and *"falling very slowly."* By contrast, my wife was not sinking; instead, her arms had become extendable. *"Look how far my arms can stretch, honey."* At some point we turned in for the night and slept like the dead. This story is foreshadowing what's to come.

My wife was a track athlete through high school. So, when any major meets are televised, the family is watching track and field. In June of 2021, the US Track & Field Olympic Trials were taking place in Eugene, Oregon. Like what I do with cycling and all the big three American sports, my wife follows the happenings of track beyond the usual four-year Olympic cycle that most casual American sports fans do. She knows the names of the athletes, both men and women, their events, and their best times. This is one of the reasons that we have been together as long as we have, and I'm damn proud of it. Knowing that my favorite track event is the 100-meters, she called me to the living room to watch a young, brash phenom from Dallas, Texas, named Sha'Carri Richardson.

The first thing that caught my attention was how much stuff she had on her person. Long, flowing orange hair, fingernails that looked to be at least two inches long, and HUGE eye lashes. As a swimmer who wanted as little drag exposed as possible, I remember asking aloud how she could concentrate with all that stuff on her body. As the fastest qualifier, Sha'Carri lined up in the lane five in the middle of the final group. The first half of her race was mediocre and by the 50-meter mark she looked to be in fourth or fifth place. But then she hit her second gear, pulling ahead with 20 meters to go, winning by what looked to be a large margin between herself and Javianne Oliver in second place. She won with a time of 10.86. Second place was 10.99. After she crossed the finish line, Sha'Carri kept running in celebration as she slung her plentiful hair all over the place and wagged her right index finger as the obvious number one US representative. I always love seeing a fellow Texan kick ass, but I loved watching Richardson even more. I enjoy a little swagger in my sporting heroines and Sha'Carri had confidence to spare.

After a quick trip into the stands to hug her grandmother and the other members of her entourage, she came down to the track and provided a post-race interview during which she revealed that her birthmother had died unexpectedly just a week prior to the trials.

> *"My family has kept me grounded. This year has been crazy for me. Going from, just last week, losing my biological mother, and I'm still here. I'm still here. Last week finding out my biological mother passed away and still choosing to pursue my dreams, still coming out here and still making sure to make the family that I do still have on this earth proud,"*

> *"Y'all see me on this track, and y'all see the poker face that I put on but nobody but them and my coach know what I go through on a day-to-day basis. I'm highly grateful for them. Without them, there would be no me. Without my grandmother, there would be no*

Sha'Carri Richardson. So, my family is my everything. My everything until the day I'm done."

The revelation about her birth mother immediately struck me. The term *"biological mother"* specifically felt intentional and a little detached. She was telling the world that it wasn't her mother who died, but rather the woman who had given birth to her. As impersonal as it felt, her mother's death had clearly had an impact on her that was palpable during the interview. I took that information and stored it in my subconscious as the coverage moved on to the next race. I was certainly looking forward to watching Sha'Carri Richardson go up against the best competition that the world had to offer in Tokyo. Unfortunately, that didn't happen.

Twelve days after she fired a warning shot across the bows of the best sprinters in the world, it was announced that Sha'Carri Richardson had tested positive for Tetrahydrocannabinol (THC), the psychoactive component of marijuana. She would be subject to a competition ban of at least one month, meaning that she would be ineligible to compete in the Tokyo Olympics. Despite the fact she had smoked marijuana in Oregon, where those over 21 years of age can legally possess, use, and purchase marijuana for recreational purposes, THC is on the WADA's banned substances list. The next day she went on the Today Show to apologize for her actions. She said that she had smoked marijuana to calm her nerves after learning that her biological mother had died. She received the horrible news from a reporter who posed the news in the form of a question, i.e., do you have any response to the fact that your mother died? What a prick...

"People don't understand what it's like to have to ... go in front of the world and put on a face and hide my pain. Who am I to tell you

how to cope when you're dealing with the pain or you're dealing with a struggle that you haven't experienced before, or that you thought you never would have to deal with?"

The public response was heavily in Richardson's favor. Under a torrent of negative responses to the story, the CEO of USADA, Travis Tygart, was forced to defend the position of USADA.

"The rules are clear, but this is heartbreaking on many levels; hopefully, her acceptance of responsibility and apology will be an important example to us all that we can successfully overcome our regrettable decisions, despite the costly consequences of this one to her."

After three years, I still can't believe how remarkably tone-deaf Tygart's response was. What exactly did Richardson have to apologize for? What had she done wrong in the eyes of WADA? Officially, marijuana is on the banned list because it is designated as a substance of abuse, and thus it violates the spirit of sport. Here begins the debate. How exactly is the consumption of a plant that grows naturally all over the planet against the spirit of sport? The theory goes that substances of abuse are antithetical to the spirit of sport which is all about health and well-being. If we are discussing harder drugs like meth, cocaine, or heroin (or it's legal cousins like Oxycontin), I would agree. But marijuana, no... I don't agree. There is a moralistic tinge to this statement that goes unspoken. Those who take **illegal** drugs are in violation of laws that were put in place to protect against a criminal element. It is the criminality of taking illegal drugs that makes them against the spirit of sport. HORSESHIT! Is my response.

If they are going to do anything, doping prevention organizations should stick to rooting out performance enhancement and leave recreational drugs, regardless of why someone wants to take them, out of consideration. This is particularly true when you look at the sponsorship agreements that exist between many sports governing bodies and alcohol producers. Hell, Asahi Breweries were the *"Official Beer Sponsor"* of the Tokyo Olympics, paying a cool $130 million for the privilege of providing their drug of abuse to anyone of legal drinking age [1]. Guess what, in 2018, WADA removed alcohol from its banned substances list, maintaining the restriction on its use to *"in competition"* only. Well, isn't that convenient, just in time to start negotiating with Asahi for the 2020 games. When you consider that alcohol is considered by most addiction specialists to be significantly more addictive than marijuana, and that both marijuana and alcohol are legal in Oregon where Richardson was competing, and the whole argument falls apart. If you can legally drink an Asahi beer the day before your competition to calm your nerves after being ambushed with the news that your mom just died, you should also be able smoke a joint!

Since I've made the case for why marijuana consumption is obviously not against the spirit of sport, that leaves two more rules that we must clear before we can expect WADA to stop wasting its time legislating the *"morality"* of athletes' behavior. Let's start with the most obvious question: is marijuana a performance enhancing drug? Although this question is still debated, most of the published data comes from the 1970s and 1980s, which tells me that the scientific community decided that this matter was largely settled between 40 and 50 years ago. After an extensive search of the relevant literature, I was able to find only four studies on the impact of marijuana on athletic performance that I felt were well designed.

- Steadward & Singh (1975). Eighteen young men who smoked marijuana regularly had their power output measured on a stationary bike while riding at a steady heart rate of 170 beats/min. Each subject was tested under three conditions; after 20-25 "toks" (their word) of marijuana, or a placebo (same plant with the THC removed), or a control session without smoking [2].

- Resting heart rate (beats/min) increased significantly after smoking marijuana (Control = 73.7, Placebo = 78.1, Marijuana = 105.8). Because of this, during exercise the subjects reached 170 beats/min at a much lower exercise intensity then they did during either the control or placebo conditions. That means that at the same heart rate their power output (kg-m/min) plummeted (Control = 1177.2, Placebo = 1099.2, Marijuana = 829.9).
- Let me put this into context. Let's say that instead of keeping the heart rate constant between each test, we asked the subjects to ride at same power output during the control condition ride, in other words the subjects would be asked to ride at a constant power of 1177.2 kg-m/min during each session and we would see how long they could ride. After smoking marijuana, the subjects fatigue much sooner after smoking marijuana because of their elevated heart rate.

- Avakian et al. (1979) [3]. Similar to the previous study, six male marijuana smokers rode on a stationary bike for 15 minutes at 50% of their maximal capacity during the same three conditions, i.e., control, placebo, or marijuana. Heart rate was significantly elevated after smoking marijuana during rest, exercise, and recovery.
- Renaud & Cormier (1986) [4]. Twelve healthy young subjects underwent two exercise tests. The control condition was without smoking marijuana and the second ride was done ten minutes after smoking a joint

(my word). The primary measure was time to exhaustion while the resistance on the bike was progressively increased. After smoking the joint, the average time to exhaustion dropped by a minute from 16.1 min to 15.1. Here again, resting heart rate was significantly increased after smoking marijuana (Control = 94.3, Marijuana = 119.0). In this case heart rate was also measured throughout the entire test to the point of exhaustion. As would be expected, smoking marijuana increased heart rate at all stages of submaximal exercise.

But athletic performance is dependent on more than just the functioning of our muscular and cardiovascular systems. Our cognitive abilities and psychological state of being are just as important. This is likely why most of the purported evidence of marijuana's performance enhancing properties come from surveys (i.e., *do you think you play better high?*), and anecdotal evidence (i.e., *dude, one time I was so stoned that I scored fifty points in a basketball game.*) But these studies are not scientific because they have no controls. When reading these reports, the recurrent hypothesis is that in the doses that athletes are assumed to ingest it (which is impossible to know for a host of reasons, e.g., individual tolerance, manner of consumption, potency of strain, etc.), THC can act as an anxiolytic drug that reduces tension and anxiety while improving concentration and focus [5, 6]. Clearly, the researchers who have reported these findings have never tried to compete in any sport after smoking, eating, or drinking weed. Back to my evening with my wife in our AirBnB in Portland. No matter how much I would have wanted to swim, run, ride, lift weights, or box, I couldn't have competed against anyone after eating those chocolates. No doubt, I had zero anxiety that night. But that's not the point. Any good athlete will tell you that they need at least some tension to perform at their best. You certainly can't be so hyped up that you're psyched out, but you also can't be so relaxed that you end up staring at your feet for three hours wondering about the ethos of toes. To that end, here is the fourth study that I found.

- Bird et al. (1980) [7]. A battery of tests was administered several times over a five-hour period following smoking marijuana. Balance, reaction time, hand-eye coordination, and cognitive recall, i.e., the ability to follow instructions and memorize patterns under duress, were all significantly impaired for the entire five-hour session following smoking.

So, let's take stock. The scientific evidence suggests very strongly that smoking marijuana impairs both the physiological and cognitive parameters of exercise performance. But there is one more point to be made about the anxiolytic properties of THC. Although I don't accept that the calming effects of marijuana are performance enhancing, it is very interesting that prescription anxiolytics like Xanax and Valium are not banned by WADA so long as they are taken with a prescription. So, if you can legally calm your nerves before a race with some Xanax, why not marijuana?

That's two of WADA's criteria for banning a drug that I've knocked down:

- Smoking a plant to alter your state of consciousness has nothing to the with the spirit of sport, and
- Marijuana is clearly not a performance enhancing drug. Let's finish the job and move on to the third and final argument as presented by Travis Tygart.

"Inclusion of Cannabinoids, including marijuana, on the Prohibited List has been vigorously debated since WADA's inception back in 2003. Many now support it being removed since the list should be primarily

about performance-enhancing substances and because marijuana is widely available in certain countries. However, many also agree from a sport health and safety standpoint that it should remain on the list to prevent possible impairment and serious injuries during competition. For example, we don't want an impaired cyclist speeding at 70 miles per hour in a group of other cyclists down a mountain in the Tour de France or a similarly impaired snowboarder risking injuries on a half-pipe at the Olympics."

Hold the fort! Did the CEO of USADA just imply that marijuana is not a performance enhancing drug? I believe he did. But I digress. Obviously, we don't want our athletes stoned, drunk, or otherwise impaired while competing. This goes without saying. But Sha'Carri Richardson was not high when she won the 100-meter dash at the Olympic trials on June 19th, 2021. According to her, and not disputed by USADA or anyone else, the last time that she smoked marijuana prior to the final heat was at least two days before. By that point any potentially dangerous effects of the THC would have worn off. She was not a danger to herself or her fellow competitors.

But his analogy raises an interesting point, and since Mr. Tygart opened the door, I'm going to take the opportunity to point out a glaring inconsistency. If WADA and USADA are so concerned about athletes' being a danger to themselves or others while under the influence of sensory impairing drugs during competition, why was Rafael Nadal allowed to completely numb his foot numerous times over a two-week span during the 2022 French Open? It appears that everyone involved in that case used their better judgement and decided that playing tennis and flying down a mountain at 70 mph on a bike are not the same thing. It could be reasonably argued that running really fast in a straight line is an even less technically challenging task than either tennis or cycling. Let me be clear: I'm glad Rafael Nadal was given the right to choose to have his foot numbed. He made a conscious decision to take the risk of further injury and then went out and won his 14th French Open. Kudos Rafa! That's how it should be! So, let's give Sha'Carri Richardson that same right. She should have been allowed to use marijuana two days before the most important race of her life to fight off the anxiety caused by losing her mother. This position is backed by logic and basic humanity.

Thankfully, the tide appears to be turning on this issue. In 2020, the MLB stopped punishing the use of marijuana outside of competition, although it still restricts players being sponsored by, or investing in, the marijuana industry [8]. That same year, the NFL removed the potential of suspension for the use of illicit drugs, not just marijuana, but fines were still possible [9]. Maintaining its traditional position as the most progressive of the three big leagues, the NBA removed marijuana from its banned substances list in 2023, effectively treating it the same as it does alcohol [10]. Even the NCAA looks to be heading in the direction of loosening its restriction on the use of marijuana by collegiate student-athletes. In June of 2023, the NCAA Committee on the Competitive Safeguards and Medical Aspects of Sports (CSMAS) recommended removing marijuana from the banned substances list [11]. How ironic that the country with some of the most restrictive and punitive laws on its books is leading the way to reforming how we perceive the relationship between illicit drugs and sports. Come on WADA, join the party. Let's have some THC-infused gummies and talk about it.

Postscript. Today is August 21, 2023. I finished this chapter yesterday. Today, Sha'Carri Richardson lined up for the women's final of the 100-meter sprint at the World Track &

Field Championships in Budapest, Hungary. Coming out of lane 9, she blazed to a personal best of 10.65 and won. Her time is tied for the fifth fastest in history. I guess that marijuana she ate two days before the final of the US Olympic Trials in 2021 wasn't performance enhancing after all because she just ran faster without it. Go figure...

Reference:

1. Bisson, M. *Asahi Breweries Signs Tokyo 2020 Sponsorship Deal.* Around the Rings, 2021.
2. Robert D. Steadward, M.S., *The Effects of Smoking Marihuama on Physical Performance.* Medicine and Science in Sports, 1975. 7(4): p. 309-311.
3. E. V. Avakian, S.M.H., E. D. Michael, S. Jacobs, *Effect of Marihuana on Cardiorespiratory Responses to Submaximal Exercise.* Clinical Pharmacology & Therapeutics, 1979. **26**(6): p. 777-781.
4. André M. Renaud, Y.C., *Acute Effects of Marihuana Smoking on Maximal Exercise Performance.* Medicine & Science in Sports & Exercise, 1986. **18**(6): p. 685-689.
5. Hilderbrand, R.L., *High-Performance Sport, Marijuana, and Cannabimimetics.* Journal of Analytical Toxicology, 2011. **35**(November/December): p. 624-637.
6. Marilyn A. Huestis, I.M., and Olivier Rabin, *Cannabis in Sport: Anti-Doping Perspective.* Sports Medicine, 2011. **41**(11): p. 949.966.
7. K. D. Bird, T.B., G. B. Chesher, D. M. Jackson, G. A. Starmer & R. K. C. Teo, *Intercannabinoid and Cannabinoid-Ethanol Interactions and Their Effects on Human Performance.* Psychopharmacology, 1980. **71**: p. 181-188.
8. Passan, J. *MLB: Players Still Subject to Penalty for Using Pot.* ESPN, 2020.

9. Thompson, J. *NFL Players Can Smoke Mmarijuana for the First Time During the Offseason and the Window Opened on 4/20*. Insider, 2021.
10. Johnson, A. *NBA Will No Longer Penalize Marijuana Use, Report Says: Here's How Other Leagues Measure Up*. Forbes, 2023.
11. Kim, J. *The NCAA Looks to Weed out Marijuana From its Banned Drug List*. NPR, 2023.

Chapter 9. Hey, you got your peanut butter in my chocolate.

*"You got your chocolate in my peanut butter." **—Reese's Commercial, 1981***

After a three-year retirement, in the fall of 2008, Lance Armstrong announced that he was returning to professional cycling. Ostensibly he was doing this to raise awareness about cancer as part of a new partnership between his Livestrong Foundation and the Clinton Global Initiative. But I didn't believe it was as altruistic as that. Like most superstar athletes, Armstrong missed the competition, and he was bored. Most of my friends who were casual cycling fans were excited. As for me, not so much. I knew that there was only one person Armstrong would allow to be his director sportif (team coach/manager), Johan Bruyneel, the same man who had been his director for all seven of his Tour wins.

The problem was that by 2008, Bruyneel had a new team leader who had already won the Tour in 2007, Alberto Contador. While my friends immediately started thinking about Lance in the Yellow jersey, I was more excited to see how the impending soap opera would play out. The Astana team that Bruyneel directed, and for which Contador had just signed a new two-year contract, wasn't going to turn down the opportunity to host the travelling circus they were about to inherit when the 37-year-old, seven-time Tour winner went up against the defending champion. Better still, Contador, ten years younger than Lance, was almost as cocky and brash as Armstrong. Contador was signed by Bruyneel to the Discovery Channel team (formerly US Postal Service Team) to be Lance's replacement. The 2009 Tour de France didn't disappoint. Although he put up one hell of a fight, the older version of Lance Armstrong was no match for the younger Contador who won his second Tour in three seasons. Lance placed a very respectable third and quickly left Astana, taking Bruyneel with him.

Lance's decision to stage a comeback in 2009 could be called romantic by fans who love those kinds of sports stories. But his decision to start a new team, with a failing RadioShack as the primary sponsor no less and race the Tour again in 2010 was pure hubris. What had been hyped for an entire year as a showdown between Armstrong and Contador became a route as Lance suffered from something he had largely avoided since his first comeback from testicular cancer in 1998, bad luck. The rider who famously swerved around a crashed Joseba Beloki and continued off-road through a field filled with large rocks before re-joining the race, now couldn't stay upright. During a mountainous stage eight, Lance crashed three times and lost 11:45 to the rest of the contenders. By contrast, Contador having another great tour, was engaged in a close battle with Luxembourger Andy Schleck, finally beating him by 39 second, one of the narrowest margins of victory in Tour de France history. But of course, that's where this story really begins.

On July 21st, 2010, the Tour was camped in Pau during the second rest day. With four stages left and only eight seconds separating Contador and Schleck, relaxation was hard to come by. The following day would be the last in the mountains and would take the peloton over three major climbs including the famed Tourmalet, one of the toughest mountains in all of cycling. Hoping to provide a happy distraction from the effort to come, Contador's team organized a dinner complete with fillet mignon from Irun, Spain, about 90 miles from Pau. The steaks were requested by the team chef who had complained about the quality of the meat in the hotel where the team was staying. The delivery was made by Spanish race organizer Jose Luis Lopez Cerron, a friend of the chef. Interestingly enough, Cerron has been the president of the Spanish cycling federation (RFEC) since 2012. At some point after dinner, Contador took a regularly scheduled doping control test, as was mandatory for whoever was wearing the race leader's Yellow jersey. The next day

Contador and Schleck finished together at the top of the Tourmalet. Two days later, Contador would pad his lead by 31 seconds during the penultimate stage of the race, a 32-mile time trial between Bordeaux and Pauillac.

Just over a month later, on August 23rd, The UCI informed Contador that his doping control test in Pau had come back positive for the drug clenbuterol [1]. The following day the UCI placed Contador under provisional suspension, meaning that although he was not considered guilty just yet, he could neither compete nor participate in team activities. When a doping test is administered, the urine sample is divided into two equal volumes, an A and B sample. The A sample is tested first. If it comes back negative for PED, that's the end of the story. If, however, it comes back positive, the athlete in question has the right to ask for the B sample to be tested as well. If the B sample comes back negative, the test is considered inconclusive, and the athlete is cleared. If the B sample is positive, that's a failed test and the punishment phase begins. Contador requested that his B sample be tested on August 24th. On September 8th, the B sample came back positive for clenbuterol.

Clenbuterol is an interesting drug. It was developed in the 1960s in Germany as a decongestant and bronchodilator for those suffering from breathing disorders including asthma and COPD [2, 3]. Clenbuterol binds to epinephrine (epi) receptors and mimics the stimulatory effects of epi throughout the body. It increases awareness, heart rate, blood pressure and body temperature. But the most interesting effect of clenbuterol is how it changes body composition. Not only does clenbuterol increase the metabolism of fat, but it also has anabolic properties that allow those who take it to increase their muscle mass. These properties made clenbuterol very popular with body builders in the 1980s. But these properties also make it indispensable to other industries. Can you guess what industry really loves these same outcomes? Animals who put on extra, lean muscle mass very quickly, reducing feed costs and speeding time to market. That's right, producers of beef, chicken, and pork love clenbuterol. Although the US banned the use of clenbuterol in animal husbandry in 1991 (the Europeans followed in 1996), it still happens frequently. The Washington Post reported in 2023 that Mexican authorities had rejected pork exports from a slaughterhouse in North Carolina because samples were contaminated with clenbuterol [4]. Can you see where this is going?

On September 30th, 2010, more than two months after winning his third Tour, Contador revealed he had tested positive for clenbuterol during the rest day in Pau and blamed the Spanish filet mignon for his positive result. This is where the story gets really crazy. A first failed drug test should have resulted in a two-year ban for Contador. But, because they believed that the clenbuterol came from contaminated beef and was not ingested with the express purpose of enhancing his performance, the RFEC initially proposed a one-year ban [1]. But this didn't happen until January 26th, 2011, four months after the test results were announced. Then, out of the blue, on February 15th, the RFEC forgot about the proposed one-year ban and cleared Contador of any wrongdoing. That allowed him to begin the new race season the next day at the Tour of Algarve in Portugal. A month later the UCI appealed to the Court of Arbitration for Sports (CAS) to overturn the RFEC's decision to clear Contador, instead seeking to have a two-year ban reinstated. Five days later, WADA also joined the case against Contador. The case wasn't heard for another eight months, during which time Contador won his second Giro d'Italia and finished fifth in the Tour. Finally, on February 6th, 2012, the CAS reinstated Contador's two-year ban and backdated it to the time that he was first provisionally suspended by the UCI, meaning that he could not compete again until August 5th, 2012, AND all his results posted during the time he was competing after eating the bad meat were forfeited, including his 2010 Tour de France title.

So, who to believe? Although the use of clenbuterol in the Spanish meat industry and the rest of the European Union, was banned in 1996, there are still unscrupulous or desperate ranchers who will use it to make more money. On October 13th, 2010, Spanish police arrested 34 people in Tenerife and Gran Canaria on suspicion of being part of an animal doping ring which was allegedly supplying clenbuterol to farmers to beef up their cattle (pun intended) [5]. Once clenbuterol enters the food chain, there can be enough of it in the meat to show up on doping control tests. During the Under-17 World Cup of Soccer hosted by Mexico in June of 2011, 109 of the players from 19 of the 24 squads tested positive for clenbuterol after consuming the food prepared at the team hotels [6]. Fédération Internationale de Football Association (FIFA), the governing body of soccer, ordered meat samples from the hotels to be tested and 30% came back positive. Ironically, none of the members of the Mexican team tested positive. It turns out that after a few of the members of the senior national team tested positive for clenbuterol after eating contaminated meat, the management only allowed the junior players to eat fish and vegetables. Thanks for the heads up, Mexico!

So, it's been established that despite being banned in animal husbandry, clenbuterol is still widely used as an anabolic agent in the meat industries of several countries. It's also clear that clenbuterol is present in meat in high enough concentrations to show up in doping control tests. That said, it's still possible that Contador took the drug to enhance his performance. The next questions to ask are:

- How much clenbuterol would be needed for performance enhancement, and
- how much clenbuterol was in Contador's urine sample.

The first question is impossible to answer because we don't have any studies to turn to, and since clenbuterol is banned for human consumption, we never will. So, we turn to the minimum level that WADA-accredited labs are required to be able to detect to be contracted as a testing facility, a concentration of 2 ng/ml. Contador's urine sample contained 50 pg/ml of clenbuterol, that's 40X less than the required minimal detection level [7]. No one disputes Contador's position that the clenbuterol had to enter his system during the second rest day on July 21st. We know this because Contador was tested for six consecutive days from July 19th-24th [8]. The only two tests that came back positive for clenbuterol were on the 21st (50 pg/ml) and the 22nd (falling to 20 pg/ml). When we take all the evidence together, there are only two logical explanations. Either Contador took just enough clenbuterol to test positive but not receive any performance enhancing benefit, or he's telling the truth, and he ate contaminated beef. Either way, it is extremely unlikely that the amount of clenbuterol in his system helped him win the Tour de France.

A little more than ten years later another elite athlete would experience a similar ordeal, with a much different outcome. Shelby Houlihan is an American middle-distance runner who holds the American record at both the 1500-meter and 5000-meter distances. She placed 11th in the 5000 at the 2016 Rio Olympics, and 4th in the 1500 at the 2019 World Championships in Qatar. On December 15th, 2020, Houlihan provided an out-of-competition urine sample that came back positive for 19-NA, a metabolite of the anabolic steroid nandrolone, a PED most commonly used by bodybuilders, but also by runners [9]. Testing of the over-the-counter supplements she was taking at the time of the failed test all came back negative. After constructing a two-week food journal, she settled on a burrito from a food truck that she ate the night before the fateful doping control test. While out to dinner with two teammates in her hometown of Beaverton, Oregon, she ordered what she thought was a carne asada (beef) burrito. Houlihan insisted that the burrito didn't taste like, or have the texture of beef, and it was so greasy and heavy that she couldn't finish it. The food truck also served pork offal, a mixture of organ meats including heart, lungs, brain, liver, cheeks, tongue, and kidney.

Like what happened with Alberto Contador, the Athletics Integrity Unit (AIU), the anti-doping arm of World Athletics, the governing body of track and field, (formerly the IAAF) placed her under provisional suspension and then took their time to come to a conclusion. After her B sample came back positive, and in the hopes of clearing her name before the US Olympic Trials, Houlihan appealed directly to CAS. The AIU called Dr. John McGlone, a food-sciences professor from Texas Tech University, who testified that the chances of an offal burrito causing a positive test for 19-NA were less than 1 in 10,000. According to McGlone, the source of the meat would have to be a boar, that was an uncastrated male with undescended testicles. Boar meet is rare in the US food chain as it enters through a different route than does domestic, farm-raised pork. Finally, all of this assumes that the food truck gave her offal instead of what Houlihan had ordered, beef.

In Houlihan's corner was Dr. Emmanuel Strahan, a former certified scientist at the WADA-certified lab in Stockholm, Sweden, who testified that Houlihan's urine samples, *"show all the evidence of boar meat or offal consumption the day prior to when the urine test was performed"*. Houlihan also hired Dr. Pascal Kintz, an independent expert in toxicology and pharmacy, to test her hair for 19-NA. When you inject steroids intramuscularly, the most common route, their levels remain elevated in the blood for weeks, if not longer. As the hair grows, it takes up the metabolites of steroids. Hair grows at roughly one cm a month. Kintz tested six cm of Houlihan's hair, representing the six-month period that included when she ate the burrito and tested positive. The tests came back negative. Just like with Contador, this means that however the nandrolone entered Houlihan's system it was likely a single pulse instead of long-term use, which is what would be expected if nandrolone were taken as a PED.

Although CAS does not report the vote of the three-member panel, it's clear from the language in the document that it was a 2-1 vote against Houlihan. This means she almost convinced them of her argument. In their summation the panel said,

> *"The Panel finds it possible but improbable that the ingestion of boar meat (cryptorchid) would have resulted in the urinary concentration found in the Athlete's A- and B-Samples [10]."*

Possible but improbable... To me, this statement sounds like reasonable doubt existed. But CAS doesn't work like a court of law. It is up to the accused to prove her innocence, not the other way around.

Interestingly, USADA CEO Travis Tygart made statements that appeared to be in support of Houlihan. Their official position is that additional investigation beyond lab results is needed in cases where only trace amounts of banned substances are found and there is a plausible, innocent explanation.

> *"We always seek justice — to do what is right given the facts — not just the blind, tone-deaf execution of WADA's sometimes unfair, ivory tower demands. Unfortunately, there is frequently a real tension between the two [9]."*

Yikes, that's some serious chin music (baseball reference meaning that the pitcher is intentionally throwing the ball close to the batter's chin.)

WADA has set the upper limit of 19-NA that an athlete can have in their urine without the test being considered positive at 2.0 ng/ml. But I found one paper that suggests that it is possible to experience urine levels above that threshold after eating bore meet. De Wasch et al. (2000) had three male volunteers eat 310 grams (about 2/3 lbs.) of a mixture of boar tissue including muscle, liver, heart, and kidney [11]. Ten hours after eating the boar products, 19-NA levels in the urine samples of the three men were 3.1, 3.7, and 7.5 ng/ml respectively. Houlihan's two samples were 6.9 and 7.8 ng/ml, above the WADA threshold but similar to what was observed by De Wasch.

Clearly there is some strong evidence to support the possibility that Houlihan is telling the truth. Just like with Contador, if she's not and she was taking nandrolone to try and gain a competitive advantage, she did it stupidly. She would have had to have injected a drug that is meant to be taken for at least a few days, if not weeks, if you want to gain a competitive advantage, only once and in a quantity that would impart no realistic benefit. Even if she had taken it to aid with recovery, she would have done so during, or immediately after the altitude training camp she travelled to in Flagstaff, Arizona in January of 2021. This is where she learned the results of her failed doping test. Instead, she would have taken it, just once, weeks before, during a period relatively low intensity training. Unfortunately, CAS didn't agree with my position and gave her a four-year competition ban, a duration designed to make sure that the offender misses at least one Olympic cycle. As fate would have it, because of the postponement of the 2020 Tokyo games, Houlihan's ban will force her to miss two Olympics. She is not eligible for competition until January 15th, 2025.

Three months before Shelby Houlihan provided her fateful out-of-competition anti-doping test, another American track star, Brenda Martinez, was caught in a similar web of intrigue, forced to prove her innocence when her sample came back positive for a drug that she said she didn't take. Martinez competed in the 2016 Rio games in the 1500-meters and won the silver medal in the 800-meter at the 2013 World Championships, ironically after Russia's Maryia Savinova was disqualified for doping.

While training for the 2020 US Olympic Trials, Martinez's urine sample tested positive for hydrochlorothiazide (HCTZ), a diuretic typically used to treat high blood pressure [12]. HCTZ is on the banned substance list because it can act as a masking agent, meaning that HCTZ may hide the presence of other banned drugs by flushing them out of the body quickly and diluting urine samples, making them other drugs harder to detect.

Following the protocol for a contested positive test, Martinez handed over all the prescription oral medications that she had registered with USADA, and that she was taking at the time of her failed test. A few agonizing months later, USADA announced that Martinez's failed test was a false-positive caused by contamination of her antidepressant that she was taking legally. Although she was relieved to have her reputation restored, she had to reveal to the world that she was taking antidepressants. At that point in her journey, only four people were aware that she was struggling with depression: her doctor, her husband, and two people at New Balance, her shoe sponsor.

> *"It was hard for me to admit I needed help, and I didn't want to add any stress to anyone else's life and worry them about me [12]."*

Martinez's antidepressants could have been contaminated during production when common vats used to formulate drugs are not adequately cleaned between uses. It could also have happened at the pharmacy. The next time you pick up a prescription, watch how the pharmacist or the pharmacy technician count out the pills as they move from the big bottles to the one that you'll take home. They pour pills into a counting tray and use a spatula to count out five pills at a time. Then they move onto the next prescription, often without cleaning either the tray or the spatula.

My wife, who worked as a pharmacy technician in college, told me that she was encouraged to reuse the little orange bottles when people didn't pick up their prescriptions. She and her coworkers would go through the prescriptions that had been sitting around for days and restock them, and then reuse the bottle for other drugs. Regardless of how it happened, Brenda Martinez didn't deserve to have to suffer through three months of stress and suspicion, and she certainly didn't deserve to have her personal health history revealed to the world. Once again, USADA openly disagreed with WADA while loudly supporting Martinez.

> *"This is our sixth no-fault case in just one year, meaning that yet another athlete has been unjustly charged with a violation and publicly recognized for ingesting a prohibited substance from a completely innocent source, such as contaminated medication, meat, or water, and despite there being no effect on performance. USADA strongly objects to this requirement under the rules and will continue to urge WADA to reform the system to be fairer for athletes [13]."*

This specific problem of athlete's failing doping control tests because of trace amounts of prohibited drugs has two underlying causes. The first problem is one that I've pointed out several times. We don't know the minimum concentration of a drug needed to provide performance enhancement. If there is clear, irrefutable evidence that the athlete took the drug with the express purpose of gaining a competitive advantage, the question is moot. If you took drug A to cheat and got caught, no matter how much is there, you have to pay the piper. But if drug A got there through no fault or negligence by the athlete, then it does matter if there is enough present to make a difference in their performance. If there is, make them wait until they test negative for the drug in question and then let them return to competition. But if the levels detected are too low to matter, the athlete should be allowed to compete immediately.

The second is the remarkable sensitivity of the tests. The problem with the earliest doping tests used between 1960-2010 was that they weren't sensitive enough to detect many PED. Athletes could drink a lot of water right before a test and dilute their urine enough to hide the drugs they were taking. When testers became aware of this practice, they stopped allowing pre-test hydration. Athletes responded by taking diuretic *"masking agents."* Even if you're a little dehydrated, if you take a diuretic, you'll make plenty enough urine to dilute your sample. When diuretics were banned, athletes switched to micro-dosing. Instead of injecting steroids or EPO into the muscle or under the skin, where they would slowly be released into the blood stream over days or weeks, athletes began injecting micro-doses directly into their veins. This gave them a small pulse of the drug that would metabolize quickly.

But now the tests are so sensitive that athletes are testing positive for banned substances that entered their body during sex with their partners. In 2020, US Olympic boxer Ginny Fuchs was cleared after trace amounts of metabolites of two banned drugs, letrozole and GW1516, were found in her urine [14, 15]. Men take letrozole to increase sperm counts, and GW1516 treats metabolic and cardiovascular diseases.

Another case was that of US Olympic softball player Madilyn 'Bubba' Nickles who tested positive for metabolites of Ligandrol, an anabolic agent taken by her partner that is commonly used to increase muscle mass [9, 15]. Those who are glass-half-full optimists will say the system worked because these women were both eventually cleared. This is true, but it took a month, during which time they were humiliated and isolated from their teammates and the sports they loved. Not to mention that they had to reveal their sexual habits and the personal health information of their partners. What would have happened had either of their partners refused to cooperate with the investigation? What if either of these ladies had engaged in a one-night stand and couldn't find the person they had sex with?

Unfortunately, this problem is likely to get worse before it gets better. Although USADA is pressing for change, WADA is slow to act. As a stopgap measure to try and reduce the number of incidences of inadvertent positive tests for clenbuterol, since 2011 the USADA website has a periodically updated its list of helpful hints on ways to avoid getting exposed to the drug [16].

To reduce your risk of unintentionally ingesting a prohibited substance through contaminated meat:

- *Choose meat from a reputable source (e.g., athlete village, hotel, etc.).*
    - **But the soccer players competing in the Under 17 World Cup in Mexico ate at their team hotels and were still served tainted beef.**
- *Inquire where meat products are sourced from at hotels and restaurants (imported meats from the United States, Europe, New Zealand, or Australia have tighter regulations and higher quality standards). Consider certified-organic meats.*
    - **Fine, but what do you expect of minors? What exactly should you do if the restaurant says that the beef came from a country other than those listed above? I've already presented evidence that farmers in the US as recently as 2020 still use clenbuterol in their cattle [4].**

- *Avoid eating liver or liver-derived products.*
    - **This one is relatively easy to follow. But I have been known to enjoy some liver and onions.**
- *Do not eat street foods.*
    - **Come on... This would eliminate so many great places to eat in any major city in Texas.**
- *Avoid eating unusual or exotic meat products.*
    - **Bread and water anyone?**
- *Consider alternative protein sources.*
    - **Nothing says protein like a nice medium rare soy burger. Yummy. (Sarcasm)**
- *Request documentation demonstrating food safety and quality standards of the meat source.*
    - **Holy hell, you cannot be serious! No one is ever going to do this. What do you do if the restaurant manager does not have the documentation or refuses to provide it?**

Too bad USADA hasn't added to the list to avoid all sexual contact with anyone, including you partner or spouse, EVER! Remember, doping control tests can happen in and out of competition. If you're not convinced that this is a real problem that needs to be addressed by WADA, think about this. In 2006 the US Geological Survey released a report that documented detectable levels of several drugs in streams, lakes, and rivers in Pennsylvania [17]. Every time you take a drug, some of it ends up in your urine, then the toilet, and finally the sewage treatment plant. Unfortunately, water reclamation plants aren't designed to remove these contaminants. The drugs find their way into our drinking water. At least two of the drugs listed are on the in-competition prohibited list, the opiate codeine, and salbutamol, an asthma medication. To date, no studies have shown that you can test positive for drugs from the amounts found in drinking water. But concern shifts to the food chain. As the concentrations of these drugs increase as you move up the food chain, it's conceivable that you can eat animal products that became contaminated with prohibited drugs after they ate smaller animals or plants, further down the food chain that were living in the water supply.

So, how to fix this problem? It all starts with the determination of minimal thresholds. If there are only trace amounts of a drug in a person's system, particularly when the drug appears only one time in a series of tests, as was the case with Alberto Contador, we must be careful to avoid destroying careers and reputations. The Ultimate Fighting Championship (UFC), in cooperation with USADA, pioneered this approach in 2019 [18]. They targeted eight specific substances that were most frequently appearing in trace amounts and were known to be contaminants in over-the-counter supplements. Threshold levels have been set for each of the substances. If a fighter tests positive for one of these drugs, and their levels are above the threshold, the normal suspension process occurs. However, if they fall below the threshold, they are allowed to continue with training and competition until the matter is resolved. Following the investigation of the positive results, and if it is determined that the fighter took the substance intentionally, or was negligent in their behavior, they may still face suspension. Instead of a black and white, guilty or innocent judgement, this approach allows for some acknowledgement of the nuance that exists in the messy lives that we all live.

Postscript: On October 12th, the UFC announced that it was not renewing its contract with USADA for anti-doping testing that is set to expire on December 31st, 2023, ending their eight-year relationship [19]. The reason for the split depends on which side you listen to, but mostly revolved around complaints from UFC fighters about how frequently and when they were tested. Under the current agreement, USADA could test athletes randomly whenever they wished, including early in the morning and even during the period immediately before the weigh-in when fighters are often trying to shed weight, not an ideal time to give a blood sample or pee in a cup. For their part USADA claims that the reason for the split centers on the return of one fighter, Connor McGregor.

McGregor broke his leg during his last fight in July 2021. After surgery to repair the damage, he left the pool of fighters who are subject to regular testing and began a long recovery during which time he put on a lot of muscle. Although there is no proof, many people, including myself, believe he likely also took anabolic steroids and perhaps HGH to assist with his recovery. Sound familiar?

After more than two years away from the Octagon, it is expected that McGregor will make his return sometime in the spring of 2024. The problem is that any athlete who removed themselves from the testing pool for any reason must return to the pool for six months and pass two doping control tests before they can fight. Neither McGregor nor the UFC wanted to wait, instead proposing he only be obligated to pass the two tests. USADA's position is that no one is above the rules. On October 8th, 2023, Connor McGregor reenrolled in the testing pool, and it is expected that his long-awaited return will happen at UFC 300 in April 2024, six months after returning to the testing pool.

UFC will now enter into an agreement with Drug Free Sport, the same company that is contracted by the NBA, NFL, MLB, and NCAA to collect blood and urine samples from its fighters. Although testing will still be handled by WADA, the banned substances list, rules, and punishments will now be handled by an "independent administrator" contracted by the UFC. It appears that the UFC wants to retain a level of control over how they test and discipline their athletes in a manner like most major American sports leagues. I expect, and hope, to see more of these decisions for different sports moving forward.

Reference:

1. Staff, R. *Timeline: Alberto Contador's Doping Case.* Reuters, 2012.
2. C. Spann, M.E.W., *Effect of Clenbuterol on Athletic Performance.* Annals of Pharmacotherapy, 1995. **29**(1): p. 75-77.
3. J. J. Choo, M.A.H., R. A. Little, N. J. Rothwell, *Anabolic Effects of Clenbuterol on Skeletal Muscle are Mediated by Beta 2-Adrenoceptor Activation.* American Journal of Physiology, 1992. **263**(1): p. E50-E56.
4. Carmen, T. *Illegal Muscle-Building Drug Found in Some U.S. Pork Exports.* Washington Post, 2023.
5. Cossins, P. *34 Arrested in Spanish Clenbuterol Investigation.* CyclingNews, 2010.
6. Association, P. *Contaminated Meat Affected More Than 100 Players at Under-17 World Cup.* The Guardian, 2011.
7. Fotheringham, W. *Alberto Contador Blames Suspect Meat for Positive Drug Test During Tour.* The Guardian, 2010.
8. Tucker, R. *Contador Tests Positive.* The Science of Sport, 2010.
9. Kilgore, A. *A Postive Test, an Infamous Burrito and a Running Career in Purgatory.* Washington Post, 2023.
10. Sport, C.o.A.f., *Arbitral Award Delivered by the Court OF Arbitration for Sport.* 2021.
11. Katia De Wasch, B.L.B., Hubert De Brabander, François Andre, and Sandra Impens, *Consequence of Boar Edible Tissue Consumption on Urinary Profiles of Nandrolone Metabolites. II. Identification and*

Quantification of 19 Norsteroids Responsible for 19-Norandrosterone and 19-Noretiocholanolone Excretion in Human Urine. Mass Communications in Mass Spectometry, 2001. **15**: p. 1442-1447.
12. Crouse, L. *Antidepressants Almost Cost This Olympian Her Career*. New York Times, 2021.
13. GQLSHARE *USADA Finds Olympian Brenda Martinez not at Fault for Positive Drug Test*. Pasadena Star-News, 2020.
14. OlympicTalk *Top U.S. Olympic Boxing Hopeful, Softball Player Cleared of Doping Violations Caused by Sex*. NBC Sports.com, 2020.
15. Bupp, P. *USADA Clears two Olympic Athletes After Positive Drug Tests, Which Were Deemed due to Having Sex With Their Respective Partners*. The Comeback, 2020.
16. USADA. *Clenbuterol and Meat Contamination*. 2016; Available from: https://www.usada.org/spirit-of-sport/clenbuterol-and-meat-contamination/.
17. Survey, U.S.G., *Concentrations of Selected Pharmaceuticals and Antibiotics in South-Central Pennsylvania Waters, March through September 2006*. 2006.
18. USADA, *UFC Anti-Doping Wallet Card 2021*, USADA, Editor. 2021.
19. Raimondi, M. *Everything to Know Regarding UFC, USADA and Conor McGregor*. ESPN.com, 2023.

Chapter 10. Everybody wants some. I want some too.

"Xentrex, it's the strongest male enhancement drug in the world, and it works!"
—Dwayne, The Rock, Johnson, SNL

My last three years as a college professor were spent at a small liberal arts school in San Antonio, Texas. I taught all the tougher courses in our kinesiology program. This meant that my office hours were frequently packed with students who needed a little extra help. I would regularly have to move the groups from my tiny office to the nearest empty classroom. During one of these impromptu group tutoring sessions, as everyone was taking out their laptops and notes, one of my students produced a brown bottle of pills, shook it once, opened it, and then popped a little orange tablet into his mouth. When he realized that I was watching him curiously, he volunteered that it was Adderall. He then asked if anyone else wanted one. I thought he was joking, but of the six other people in the room, five affirmed. All five students popped their pills and waited for me to get started. It all happened so fast that I was left staring at them with my already prominent eyebrows raised several inches off my head.

All I could think to ask was whether any of them had a prescription for Adderall. All of them, including the young man whose bottle it was said no. He had purchased the bottle from an old high school friend who had stopped taking the drug years before but would still regularly fill his prescription and sell the pills. It would be another 20 minutes of conversation before I started reviewing the material for our class. Instead, we talked about why they chose to self-medicate with Adderall even though none of them had either been tested for, or diagnosed with, attention deficit disorder. The stories were consistent. Adderall helped them focus, quieting most distractions, making them feel more confident in their ability to learn.

I found these spontaneous admissions fascinating and I wanted to collect some more, informal data. I typed out a three-question survey and gave it to each of my four classes, making sure that students who were in more than one of my classes answered only once. Here is what the survey asked.

I am collecting some preliminary data for a potential research project. ***Please DO NOT write your name or any other identifying information on your paper.*** *After you answer the questions, please fold the page twice and place it in the cardboard box at the back of the class. If you do not want to participate, leave your survey blank, fold it twice and put it in the box.*

- *Have you ever taken Adderall, Ritalin, or other drugs used to treat ADD or ADHD?*
- *If you answered yes to the previous question, do you have a prescription for the drugs that you have taken?*
- *Why did you take the drug without a prescription?*
- *Please add anything else that you think I should know below this space.*

Of the 58 students in my four classes, 53 were present and willing to answer my questions. Four students were absent on the day I passed out the survey. Only one left the survey blank. Of the 53 who participated, 15 (28%) admitted to taking either Adderall or Ritalin without a prescription. Four other students had a prescription for Adderall. The reasons why they took these stimulants all revolved around their desire to focus so they could get better grades. But there were three students who wrote about taking Adderall because it made them more confident with the opposite sex.

My first question was why my study group was not representative of all my students. Five of six students (83%) in that first group took an Adderall right in front of me. A quick mental attendance check of those six students answered my question. All six people in the first study group were A students. Just like with parent-teacher conferences when I was a high school math and science teacher 20 years earlier, when most of the parents who attended were those of the A and B students, my office hours' attendees were almost without exception the best of my students. These students represented the most driven, ambitious, and competitive of their peers. Not surprisingly, all six of these students were also scholarship athletes.

The day after collecting data for my non-scientific survey, I shopped the results around to several of my faculty colleagues and two administrators. It was universally met with shoulder shrugs. No one thought it was particularly interesting and everyone said there was little that anyone could, or would, do about it. The story is the same across the country, particularly with college and graduate students. Studies have shown that the rate of college students using Adderall or similar drugs without a prescription is between 5% and 35%, and that college-aged students are twice as likely to misuse the drug than their non-student peers [1, 2].

A few weeks later, my family and I attended a birthday party for one of my daughter's classmates at our neighborhood pool. With all the kids occupied, the parents began exchanging work stories. I brought up my Adderall story. As I expected, no one found the results either surprising or concerning. Three people even admitted to regularly taking Adderall during periods of high work stress, or as one of them called it, *"deadline season."* One of those people had convinced her doctor to give her a prescription for Adderall, even though she didn't have any diagnosed issue with attention deficits. The other two got their supplies from an assortment of sources, all illegal.

After meandering through several other mundane topics, the conversation found its way to tennis. Somehow, we began talking about the Russian former tennis star Maria Sharapova. The person who had the prescription for Adderall, we'll call her Margo, is also a tennis player. Margo told us the story of how Sharapova had been banned for two years after taking the drug Meldonium. As the story goes, Sharapova had been taking the drug, with a prescription, for at least ten years to treat a supposed heart condition [3]. When she tested positive for it in January 2016 during the Australian Open, Meldonium had been on the banned substances list for only a month. When I asked Margo what she thought about the circumstances of Sharapova's suspension, she made it clear that she thought that Sharapova deserved her punishment and that anyone who *"cheats the system deserves to be banned."* When I asked how Sharapova's circumstances were different from her own use of Adderall to improve her work performance, it took her a while to find an answer.

Not surprisingly, using Adderall to improve one's note taking skills, or make it easier to talk to girls (or boys) at parties is not unique. There are many examples of prescription drugs being taken off label and without a prescription to enhance performance in various activities. β-blockers, which are used to treat high blood pressure, attach to receptors on the heart, slowing heart rate and reducing the force with which the heart contracts. These properties make β-blockers a particularly useful PED for those whose occupation requires steady hands, for example, musicians. In 2015, the International Conference for Symphony Orchestra Musicians (ICSOM) surveyed 447 musicians about their use of β-blockers to combat performance anxiety and maintain steady hands while playing [4]. Seventy-two percent of those polled said they had tried β-blockers, and 66% of respondents said that the drugs had been either somewhat or very effective.

Back to the kid's birthday party. After a long silence, Margo finally had an answer for why her use of Adderall at work was different than Maria Sharapova's use of Meldonium to improve her endurance during tennis matches. Margo said that sports should be played on a level playing field because they are not only competing for titles, but prize money and endorsement deals. I reminded her that she had informed all of us that her hard work had led her to get a substantial bonus, a handsome raise, and that she was now in line for a vice president position. When I asked, she confirmed that there were two other people up for the same promotion. Make no mistake, it was a competition, and Margo was going to do whatever she felt necessary to win. Just like an elite athlete would. She grudgingly conceded my point but made sure to get in the last word. *"It's still different!"*

But it's not different. Musicians compete for their positions just like football players trying to make a 53-man roster in the NFL. A symphony orchestra is arranged in a hierarchy based on talent. Professional musicians audition for a limited number of chairs just like professional football players tryout for a limited number of roster spots. The higher you are in the hierarchy, the more money you make. For example, the violin section is divided into two groups, the first and second violins. Each group is then arranged from first to last chair. The difference in pay between the violinists in different ranks can be substantial. The first chair violin (also called the Concert Master) of the Dallas Symphony Orchestra made $333,355 in 2021. The second chair (Co-Concert Master) made $209,935 [5]. These are two accomplished professionals whose performances I couldn't tell apart if my life depended on it, and one makes almost 60% more than the other. Just imagine what the last chair of the second violins makes. Likely more than I do, but you get the point. Is it any wonder that two thirds of all orchestral musicians polled used a PED to help them attain their lifelong goals? No more so than it is when an athlete does it.

Let me walk you through a quick comparison of the two professions. Although there are currently no players in the NFL who did not attend at least some college, over 50% of players never finish their degrees [6]. Many of those who do are steered to one of a handful of really marketable majors by their coaches or administrators. These include subjects like liberal arts, communications, and my all-time favorite, exploratory/general studies [7]. Can you say, *"would like some fries with that?"* Don't be offended, I'm a kinesiologist and that subject is firmly entrenched in the top ten of jock majors. The point being, regardless of what it says on their transcripts, most NFL players majored in football in college.

Every year around one quarter of the approximately 73,712 college football players across all three divisions of the NCAA become eligible for the draft [8]. The NFL has 32 teams, each with 53 roster spots. When you consider that the attrition rate is around 44% from year to year, that gives us 746 spots that need to be filled [9]. Thus, the average football player has no better than a 4.6% chance to land their dream job for which they've trained a lifetime.

How do orchestra musicians stack up? Just as with football, if you want to be an orchestra musician you had better have spent most of your formative years preparing for it, specifically you need a degree in music performance. Of course, in this case graduation isn't optional like it is with football. Well over 99% of all musicians employed by orchestras have a degree in music performance [10]. In 2021, there were 7,335 music performance degrees awarded in the US [11]. In addition to the "Big Five" symphony orchestras, i.e., New York, Philadelphia, Boston, Chicago, and Cleveland, I added to my analysis the National Symphony Orchestra in Washington DC and 32 others that generated more than a million dollars in revenue in 2020 [12]. This gives us 38 major symphonies, each with, on average, 95 musicians. However, unlike professional football, symphony orchestras have much lower rates of attrition. Career-ending symphonic injuries have decreased dramatically since they eliminated full contact hitting in the orchestra pit. On the day that I'm writing this in the fall of 2023, there are 83 open positions across all 38 major orchestras. On average, each new music performance graduate has at best a 1.1% chance of landing one of these top tier jobs. Of course, there are many other smaller, less renowned orchestras in the country, just as there are secondary and tertiary football leagues, i.e., the UFL and Arena League, but no one watches that nonsense, and we all know it.

Isn't it interesting how these two seemingly disparate occupations have so much in common? Each requires years of sacrifice, dedication, and specialization to the point that its participants have extremely limited options to pursue other career paths if their dream jobs don't come to fruition. More surprising is how much more competitive the world of symphony musicians' is than the NFL. A prospective professional football player is at least four times more likely to join an NFL squad than a new graduate is to join a major symphony orchestra. But the similarities breakdown when we look at the prevalence of doping, i.e., the use of PED in each profession. A 2009 survey of retired NFL players revealed that 9.1% of the 2,552 former players surveyed admitted to using steroids, the most frequently used class of PED in the league [13]. This is in stark contrast to the 72% of ICSOM members who admitted to using β-blockers.

So why does society accept the use of PED in one highly competitive occupation but not another? Let's look again at the three questions that are asked when assessing whether or not a drug should be placed on the banned substances list.

- Do β-blockers have the potential to enhance the performance of orchestra musicians? **Absolutely**. Taking a drug that decreases the fight-or-flight response is an obvious benefit to anyone who needs to perform on stage in front of a large audience.
- Does the use of β-blockers pose a risk to the health of the musicians who use them? **Of course**. The most common side effects of β-blockers include dizziness, fatigue, and blurred vision. But some people with unusually low heart rate and blood pressure can have severe reactions to taking β-blockers.
- Is it against the spirit of the competition among musicians for someone to take β-blockers to gain an

advantage over their fellow competitors? I give this one a big shoulder shrug and a loud **"MEH!"**

Since I only need one of these three to be true, I've already demonstrated that when musicians take β-blockers to perform better than their peers, it is the exact same thing as a professional football player taking steroids to win. So, I don't really care if it's against someone else's definition of the spirit of sport, music, of any other competition in the C-suite of corporate America. In both cases the practitioners are, first and foremost, entertainers. I watch sports to see the best athletes in the world do things that I could never do myself. That's the same reason that I go to the symphony and the opera. Do I really care that the fifth cello took β-blockers or some other PED to make them play better? Not particularly. But I do respect the fact that they went the extra mile to ensure that their performance was better than it would have been otherwise. I feel the same about Max Scherzer receiving a cortisone injection in his neck before game seven of the 2019 World Series, or Rafael Nadal having his foot numbed for two weeks during the 2022 French Open, or when Andy Pettitte injected himself with HGH to try and salvage his season, or finally, when Sha'Carri Richardson smoked some weed to calm her nerves a few days before she won the 100 meter dash at the 2020 US Track & Field Olympic Trials.

I subdivided my defense of doping into four categories. Three of the positions that I've taken are easily defensible. Some banned substances have legitimate therapeutic uses that can speed recovery from injury, and their use should be regulated the same across all sports. Cortisol is a good example. Those caught with miniscule amounts of PED in their blood or urine who can make a reasonable argument for contamination or accidental consumption should be forgiven and allowed to compete immediately. Lastly, recreational drugs that do not have performance enhancing properties, e.g., marijuana, should not be on the banned substances list.

But it's the last argument that is the toughest to make. Even when an athlete takes PED intentionally for the purpose of enhancing their performance, there must be enough room in our hearts for understanding and forgiveness. This is particularly true when we look at all the examples of the PED that regular Americans take every day. Be it β-blockers for orchestra musicians or over-the-counter testosterone boosters for men of a certain age, most of us are happy to enhance our own performances with a drug while at the same time wagging a finger of self-righteous indignation at those athletes who fall short of our expectations.

So, what's the answer to addressing those who choose to dope? Although I'm not sure it's for the All-Drug Olympics to become a reality, I do know that the current punishments used by WADA are too severe. Considering a ban of 2-4 years for a first offense is almost guaranteed to end the careers of most athletes, it appears that WADA is mostly interested in eliminating the offenders from competitive existence while sending a clear message of deterrence to everyone else watching. The problem is deterrence rarely works to stop bad behavior. If it did, World Athletics wouldn't have over 550 athletes currently occupying their ineligible list. By contrast, the punishments used by the four American major sports leagues are designed to punish and then rehabilitate (Table 5). Both the NFL and MLB require all suspended players to complete a substance abuse program before they can be reinstated [14, 15]. The NBA and NHL have yet to implement similar programs, but their respective players associations have advocated for them to be added to their next collective bargaining agreements.

Table 5. Length of PED Suspension for the Four American Major Leagues and the World Antidoping Agency

Offense	WADA	NFL	NBA	MLB	NHL
First	2-4 year Ban*	6 Games	25 Games	80 Games	20 Games
Second	Lifetime	17 Games	55 Games	162 Games	60 Games
Third		≥ 2 Seasons	2 Seasons	Lifetime	≥ 2 Seasons
Fourth		Lifetime	Lifetime		Lifetime

* WADA punishments are intended to make an athlete miss one Olympic cycle. If a 2-year ban will accomplish this then this is the normal punishment for a first offense. However, it could be more if the next Olympics is more than 2 years after the offense.
An NFL season is 17 games long.
Both the NBA & NHL seasons are 82 games long.
An MLB season is 162 games long.

If you think that the lengths of the suspensions are too short, consider what it would be like for you to lose 25%-50% of your salary overnight. Why do our major sports leagues have such different ideas about how to handle PEDs? Some of it is our innate desire to not be told what to do by foreigners with the games that we invented (yes, hockey was invented in Canada but that's close enough). But the other important factor that shouldn't be ignored is the influence of unionized labor. Each of these leagues has a players' union that periodically negotiates with ownership, mostly on subjects like the split of revenue, player benefits and pensions, and also PED policy. None of the other major sports that I have written about, i.e., cycling, track and field, and tennis have anything like this. Considering it's the athletes who risk their lives to compete, perhaps it's time that they have their own representation to negotiate the terms of their labor?

As I've said throughout, sport is a metaphor for life, and that metaphor extends to the use of PED. The next time you watch TV, take note of all the commercials you see for over-the-counter supplements and, to a greater extent, prescription drugs. Of the prescription drugs in the top ten for advertising spending in 2022, four treat Type II diabetes, a disease of excess that has increased exponentially in our country over the last four decades as we have become lazier, fatter, and more gluttonous [16]. The overwhelming majority of Americans suffering from Type II diabetes could rid themselves of the disease entirely if they committed to lifestyle changes including healthier eating and regular exercise. But taking a pill is always easier than hard work. Knowing that this attitude is pervasive, pharmaceutical companies are all too happy to continue marketing their drugs that make our lives easier. This is the definition of taking a short cut. Unlike what happens when elite athletes take PED, i.e., they actually train much harder than they could without them, these Type II diabetes drugs allow the consumer to change nothing and still become at least a little healthier. This is the ultimate example of performance enhancing drugs. No need to change anything, just pop this little pill. Our athletes see these same commercials. They experience the same influences as the rest of us. Is it really logical to expect them to be immune to the promise of a better them if we are not?

Reference:

1. Levin, E. *Easy Access, Pressure on Students Contributes to Increase in Non-Prescribed Adderall Use*. 2023; Available from: https://psych.wisc.edu/news/easy-access-pressure-on-students-contributes-to-increase-in-non-prescribed-adderall-use:~:text=Studies%20show%205%20to%2035,students%20in%20their%20age%20group.&text=Because%20Adderall%20is%20a%20stimulant,a%20stronger%20effect%20while%20drinking.
2. Lian-Yu Chen, R.M.C., Eric C. Strain, G. Caleb Alexander, Christopher Kaufmann, and Ramin Mojtabai, *Prescriptions, Nonmedical Use, and Emergency Department Visits Involving Prescription Stimulants*. Journal of Clinical Psychiatry, 2016. 77(3): p. e297-e304.
3. Bonifield, J. *Meldonium: The Drug That Got Maria Sharapova Suspended From Tennis*. CNN Health, 2016.
4. Beder, J., *The 2015 Musician's Health Survey*. 2015, The International Conference for Symphony Orchestra Musicians.
5. Association, D.S., *Form 990: Return of Organization Exempt From Income Tax*, Treasury, Editor. 2021.
6. *NFL Players: Higher College Graduation Rate Than Rest of World*. 2004, National Football League.
7. Geiser, B. *These are the Most Popular Majors for College Football Players*. Sportscasting, 2019.
8. *Football: Probability of Competing Beyond High School*. 2019, National Collegiate Athletics Assoication.
9. Fitzgerald, J. *OverTheCap.com*. Roster Turnover in the NFL 2022; Available from: https://overthecap.com/roster-turnover-in-the-

nfl#:~:text=On%20average%20only%2056%25%20of,a%20team%20by%20team%20basis.&text=Avg.,-Avg.&text=So%20about%20a%20quarter%20of,a%20year%20is%20around%2070%25.

10. Zuckerman, B., *Is College Necessary for a Music Career?*, in *Music School Central*. 2019.
11. Hidalgo, C., *General Music Performance*, D. USA, Editor. 2021.
12. Andrea Suozzo, A.G., Ash Ngu, and Brandon Roberts. *ProPublica* Nonprofit Explorer 2023; Available from: https://projects.propublica.org/nonprofits/.
13. Lite, J. *NFL Players Who Use Steroids Have More Injuries*. Scientific American, 2009.
14. MLBPA, M., *Major League Baseball's Joint Drug Prevention and Treatment Program*, M.L.B.M.L.B.P.s. Association, Editor. 2022.
15. NFLPA, N., *Policy on Performance-Enhancing Substances 2023*, N.F.L.N.F.L.P. Association, Editor. 2023.
16. Statista. *Leading Pharmaceutical Brands in the United States in 2022, by National TV Ad Spend*. 2022; Available from: https://www.statista.com/statistics/639356/tv-advertise-drugs-usa/.

Appendix I: The Climb Score explained.

The Official History of the Tour de France lists 14 climbs categorized as HC by ASO [2]. Of these, the Pla d'Adet has the lowest Climb Score (87.69), which serves as the lower limit for the AC designation. For context, from a list of nine less frequently traversed climbs that have been categorized as HC by ASO at least once (Table 1), only one, the Ballon d'Alsace (70.52), would not be categorized as an AC climb using the Climb Score [3].

To establish the lower limit of Category 4, I looked at the racecourse for the 1910 Tour de France, the first Tour to include both the Alps and Pyrenees in the race route. The smallest climb in 1910 was the Col de Bayard, with a Climb Score of 28.40: this set the lower limit for Category 4. To determine the range of each category between 4 and 1, the difference in Climb Scores between the easiest AC climb (87.69), and the easiest Category 4 climb (28.40) was divided by four, giving an interval of 14.82. Finally, I set three qualifying rules to further standardize the inclusion and exclusion criteria for each major climb listed in the historical record for all Tours de France from 1903-2023. If a climb did not meet all three for the following criteria it was not considered a major climb and was excluded from the analysis.

- The horizontal distance of the climb must be at least 3.0 km from the base to its peak.
- The climb must have a minimum average grade of 3%.
- The climb must have a Climb Score of at least 28.4, i.e., equivalent to the Climb Score for the Col de Bayard, the smallest climb traversed during the 1910 Tour.

List of 14 classic Hors Category (HC) as designated by the Tour de France. Additional nine less frequently used climbs also considered "classic" by race organizers ASO.

Climb Name	First Year (Category)	Elevation (m)	Distance (km)	Grade (%)	Climb Score
Alpe d'Huez	1952 (1)	1996	16.4	7.8	127.92
Col du Tourmalet	1910 (NC)[#]	2115	18.9	7.4	139.86
Col du Galibier	1947 (1)	2642	35.1	5.5	193.05
Col de la Madeleine	1969 (2)	1993	25.3	6.5	164.45
Col d'Aubisque	1947 (1)	1709	37.7	3.7	139.49
Col de las Croix-de-Fer	1947 (1)	2064	22.7	7	158.9
Luz Ardiden	1985 (HC)	1718	14.2	7.7	109.34
Col d'Izoard	1922 (NC)[#]	2360	34.3	4.3	147.49
Col de Joux-Plane	1978 (1)	1691	12.9	7.6	98.04
Plateau de Beille	1998 (HC)	1788	15.9	7.8	124.02
Mont Ventoux	1951 (1)	1912	21.4	7.5	160.5
Pla d'Adet	1974 (1)	1680	11.1	7.9	87.69
La Plagne	1987 (HC)	2093	20.1	7	140.7
Hautacam	1994 (HC)	1615	15.9	7.6	120.84
Col de Sarenne	2013 (HC)	1999	22	5.8	127.6
Col du Lautaret	1950 (2)	2057	34.1	3.9	132.99
Col du Glandon	1947 (3)	1924	19.8	7.3	144.54
Col de l'Iseran	1938 (NC)[#]	2770	46.9	4.2	196.98
Col de la Bonette	1962 (1)	2802	25.4	6.5	165.1
Cormet de Roselend	1979 (1)	1968	20.2	6.1	123.22
Col du Soulor	1973 (1)	1474	28.9	4.1	118.49
Superbagneres	1961 (1)	1798	17.2	6.8	116.96
Ballon d'Alsace*	1905 (2)	1175	16.4	4.3	70.52

*Ballon d'Alsace is the only one of these classic climbs that would not be considered an AC climb using the Climb Score ranking system.

[#]NC means Not Categorized. The first category system wasn't created until the 1947 Tour de France.

Catalogue of Major Climbs

Next I went through archived race maps [4], to catalogue each major climb for all race routes of the Tour de France from 1903-2023. Since most climbs have multiple approaches, providing different lengths and average grades, the exact approach was determined for each year using the Cyclingcols.com website (Powered by STRAVA) [5]. For example, Mont Ventoux can be approached from three directions, i.e., from the east starting in the town of Sault (Climb Score = 115.2), from the south starting in the town of Bedoin (Climb Score = 160.5), and from the west starting in the town of Malaucene (Climb Score = 158.25). For climbs not listed in the Cyclingcols.com database, (fewer than 5% of the climbs analyzed), I used Google maps to measure both the horizontal distance from the base of the climb to its peak, and the elevation change over that distance. From those two values, I calculated the average gradient of the climb by dividing the change in elevation by the horizontal distance travelled. Each climb was then placed into one of the five categories by its respective Climb Score. The cumulative Climb Score for each year's race was calculated as the sum the individual climbs. Finally, the total number of climbs in each category was counted.

Average Speed

Using archived data from the official Tour de France website [6], the distance of each year's race route, and the winning time for each competitor was recorded. For years when disqualifications occurred, e.g., Lance Armstrong's wins in the 1999-2005 Tours, data from Bike Race Info was used [4]. The average speed for each winner, and the entire field, was calculated as the quotient of the total race distance in kilometers and the total time in hh.oo. For example, the 2021 Tour was 3383 kilometers and was won by Tadej Pogacar in a time of 82:56:36, which converts to 86.94 hours. 3383 kilometers ÷ 86.94 hours = 40.79 km/h.

Appendix II: Average attendance and total HR hit from 1990-2008.

Year	Attendance	Total HR Hit
1990	26,044	3058
1991	27,002	3383
1992	26,529	3038
1993	30,964	4030
1994 (**112**)*	31,256	3306 (**4686**)#
1995 (**144**)*	25,021	4081 (**4589**)#
1996	26,509	4962
1997	27,876	4640
1998	29,030	5064
1999	28,887	5528
2000	29,377	5693
2001	29,881	5458
2002	28,006	5059
2003	27,831	5207
2004	30,075	5451
2005	30,816	5017
2006	31,306	5017
2007	32,696	5386
2008	32,382	4878

*There are 162 games in a baseball season. During the two stroke-shortened seasons of 1994 and 1995 there were **112** and **144** games respectively. #The numbers in black are the actual totals for HR hit during the two strike-shortened seasons of 1994 and 1995. The numbers in **bold** are the extrapolated, estimated totals, i.e., if the 1994 season hadn't been cancelled there would have been around 4686 based on the pace of HR hit through 112 games. [1]

Reference:

1. Forman, S. *Baseball Reference*. 2000-2023; Available from: https://www.baseball-reference.com/leagues/majors/misc.shtml.

Appendix III: Career statistics for Andy Pettitte.

Year	Team	Games Played	Wins	Losses	Win %	ERA
1995	NYY	31	12	9	57.1	4.17
1996	NYY	35	21	8	72.4	3.87
1997	NYY	35	18	7	72.0	2.88
1998	NYY	33	16	11	59.3	4.24
1999	NYY	31	14	11	56.0	4.70
2000	NYY	32	19	9	67.9	4.35
2001	NYY	31	15	10	60.0	3.99
2002*	NYY	22	13	5	72.2	3.27
2003	NYY	33	21	8	72.4	4.02
2004*	HOU	15	6	4	60.0	3.90
2005	HOU	33	17	9	65.4	2.39
2006	HOU	36	14	13	51.9	4.20
2007	NYY	36	15	9	62.5	4.05
2008	NYY	33	14	14	50.0	4.54
2009	NYY	32	14	8	63.6	4.16
2010	NYY	21	11	3	78.6	3.28
2012	NYY	12	5	4	55.6	2.87
2013	NYY	30	11	11	50.0	3.74
Career Avg.	--	29.5	14.2	8.5	62.6	3.80

*Pettitte suffered injuries to the same elbow flexor tendon in his pitching arm, a strain in 2002 and a partial tear in 2004.

Made in the USA
Columbia, SC
10 February 2025

53636369R00102